PROMOTING SEX EQUALITY

This book is to be returned on
or before the date stamped below

− 9 NOV 1999	1 1 JAN 2001
2 4 NOV 1999	1 1 JUN 2001
− 4 MAY 2000	2 2 NOV 2001
2 5 MAY 2000	1 4 DEC 2001
1 4 NOV 2000	30 SEP 2002
− 5 DEC 2000	1 7 NOV 2003
1 5 DEC 2000	1 9 DEC 2003

PROMOTING SEX EQUALITY
The Role of Industrial Tribunals

GERALD CHAMBERS
with **CHRISTINE HORTON**

Policy Studies Institute

PSI Publications are obtainable from all good bookshops, or by visiting the Institute at 100 Park Village East, London NW1 3SR (01-387 2171).

Sales Representation: Pinter Publishers Ltd.

Individual and Bookshop orders to: Marston Book Services Ltd, PO Box 87, Oxford, OX4 1LB.

A CIP catalogue record of this book is available from the British Library

PSI Research Report 711

ISBN 0 85374 411 4

Typeset by Policy Studies Institute

Printed in Great Britain by BPCC Wheatons Ltd, Exeter

Contents

Acknowledgements

This research has been funded by the Equal Opportunities Commission and the Economic and Social Research Council.

We are indebted to Alice Leonard for her contribution to the research proposal on which this research is based. Along with others at the EOC, she continued to offer helpful advice during the course of the research, as a member of the research steering group.

The case studies on which this research is based were carried out by Gerry Chambers and Christine Horton.

The research could not have been conducted without the agreement and active involvement of the employers and members of their staffs who agreed to take part. We are greatly indebted to all those who offered us their time and extended us their facilities. Many individual industrial tribunal applicants also gave us their time and assistance, and their involvement in the project added much to the richness of the data we collected.

We would like to acknowledge the assistance we have received from staff of the Central Office of Industrial Tribunals and its various Regional Offices.

Finally, we are grateful for the comments and advice on earlier drafts we have received from various colleagues at PSI, including Bill Daniel, David Smith and Christopher McCrudden.

1 Introduction

Aims and objectives

Under the Sex Discrimination Act 1975 (SDA) and the Equal Pay Act 1970 (EqPA) individuals who feel that they have been discriminated against in employment because of their sex can seek redress at an industrial tribunal. Any such individual is free to seek advice, assistance or even legal representation in pursuing a case against an employer. The Equal Opportunities Commission (EOC) was established under the SDA and has the discretion to assist individuals to take cases of sex discrimination and equal pay to an industrial tribunal. The power to grant either advice, or assistance, or legal representation is contained in section 75 of the SDA. This section authorises the EOC, if it so wishes, to grant assistance when a case raises a question of principle, or when it would be unreasonable to expect the applicant to deal with the case unaided (either because of the complexity of the case, or because of difficulties experienced by the applicant), or for some other special reason. The EOC's powers to assist applicants are therefore discretionary, and in any case the Commission does not have the financial resources to provide legal assistance to all those who require it. Therefore the level of support provided by the Commission is not necessarily a reflection of the Commission's views on the strength or weakness of the applicant's claims, although such inferences are frequently made by both employers and applicants.

An individual's application to an industrial tribunal is essentially his or hers alone, is confined to the circumstances of the alleged act of discrimination or unfair treatment, and does not extend beyond the act complained of to a wider investigation of the employment practices of the employer cited by the applicant. This indeed is what was

1

intended by the legislation, and it was left to the EOC through a process of persuasion, education, investigation and advice to bring about wider improvements in employment practices which would have the effect of removing obstacles and promoting greater employment opportunities for women.

Nevertheless it seems reasonable to expect that individual litigation by applicants might lead an employer to remedy those aspects of policy and practice which gave rise to the discriminatory activity, and might prompt the employer to look at omissions or defects in procedures especially where these had given rise to the complaint from the applicant.

Although some internal scrutiny and reflection is likely as a result of a complaint raised by an applicant (even if that complaint is later withdrawn, settled or lost at tribunal), specific follow-up action by an employer seems most likely in cases where discrimination has been proved, and where the employer is required to make some form of compensation to the applicant.

This research investigates the extent to which an application which has been successful under either the SDA or the EqPA has been effective in eradicating the causes of the grievance, and in bringing about greater equality of treatment for men and women in the organisation concerned. It therefore focuses on those employers who having been brought before tribunals by individual applicants, have had a finding made against them, and examines their employment practices before and after the tribunal hearing. It is quite possible that a finding of discrimination or unfair treatment made against one employer, especially if that decision has been widely reported or commented on in the media, could be picked up and used constructively by another employer. Indeed the series of leaflets produced by the EOC ('Sex Discrimination Decisions') is designed to produce just such an impact. However, we are not concerned here with the wider effects of an industrial tribunal decision on other employers, although this aspect will be an important consideration in any overall assessment of the value of individual litigation.

In this research study we seek to provide answers to the following questions:

1) is the system of legal enforcement through industrial tribunals also an effective way of getting employers to examine their equal opportunity policies and practices and make appropriate changes?

2) is the tribunal decision effective in encouraging employers to remove the factors, or alter the practice or procedure, which caused the initial discrimination?
3) what factors contribute to a tribunal decision being utilised in a progressive manner by an employer?

Answers to these questions may make an important contribution to any wider evaluation of current strategies for tackling employment discrimination through legislative intervention. In particular, the findings of this research may help identify current weaknesses in the industrial tribunal system by drawing attention to missed opportunities for intervention by regulatory agencies, and to ways in which present structures could be used to greater effect. Many commentators question whether current legislative arrangements are tough enough to eradicate persistent and pervasive employment inequality between men and women, or are capable of creating better employment opportunities for women, or are targeted in such a way as to bring about real pay parity between the sexes. But what can be done within the constraints of the present framework to make the mechanisms which we have work more effectively?

The research may therefore assist in providing solutions to a broad range of operational questions. Is special training in discrimination law for tribunal members likely to produce qualitatively better decisions? Are well-reasoned decisions more effective than badly reasoned ones in promoting organisational change? Does representation make a difference to the quality of the employer's response, and if so, should representation be more widely available and legally aided? Does the intervention of the EOC influence the likelihood of the decision being put to broader effect, and if so, should the EOC intervene more often and with what resources? Can employers be expected to give wider effect to decisions without greater intervention by the EOC? Should available resources be devoted to other methods of combatting employment discrimiation against women, such as strategic investigations of employers, and should resources be diverted from support for individual litigation to these other methods? In sum, are there ways in which the tribunal system can be made to operate so as to have greater impact, or do we have to accept that its effectiveness has to be judged only in so far as it resolves individual employment grievances?

In focusing on employers' reactions to, and action taken as a result of, tribunal decisions we look at various dimensions of change from the general and qualitative to the specific and perhaps more easily measurable. First, how has the decision affected the attitude of the employer and his general receptivity towards the promotion of equality of opportunity? Is it possible to detect any heightened sensitivity, or greater awareness, or any move towards more progressive ways of thinking? Or has the decision had the reverse effect and made the employer more entrenched in his attitudes? Secondly, has the decision led the employer to introduce an equal opportunity policy, or where an equal opportunity policy statement already exists, has it led the employer to review the operation of that policy? Thirdly, has the employer taken any specific course of action designed to prevent a similar incident of discrimination or unfair treatment re-occurring? Fourthly, have any actions been taken to deal with those who were judged to be responsible for the discriminatory behaviour. And finally, where recommendations were made by a tribunal to an employer were these recommendations implemented?

Background issues
In recent years the volume of information about the workings of industrial tribunals in discrimination cases has greatly increased. But there is nothing in the currently available literature to suggest that industrial tribunals are having any effect at all on wider employment practices.

We can note first that the most recent statistics on industrial tribunal applications published by the Department of Employment for the period April 1985 to March 1987[1] continue to show that the success rate for applicants at industrial tribunals in discrimination cases is very low, and that the majority of cases are either withdrawn or settled prior to coming to the tribunal. In fact, the number of both equal pay and sex discrimination applications increased sharply in 1986-87 compared with 1985-86, but the success rate of cases reaching tribunal declined. Twenty-two per cent of sex discrimination applications were successful in 1986-87 (compared with 25 per cent the previous year, and 27 per cent for the period 1976-83 examined by Leonard).[2] Of equal pay applications, 27 per cent were successful at tribunal in 1986-87, compared with 52 per cent in 1985-86 and 19 per cent for the period 1976-83.[3] This means that for 1986-87 only

8 per cent of all sex discrimination applications and 8.5 per cent of equal pay applications resulted in success at an industrial tribunal. There has, however, over recent years been an increase in the number of cases which are settled before coming to tribunal.

Secondly, recent research[4] has cast doubt on the extent to which even the small proportion of cases which are won by applicants can be called real victories. The amount of compensation received by applicants was low, and frequently did not offset expenses incurred in pursuing a case. In addition, obtaining compensation from the employer was not always an easy matter. Applicants suggested that workplace relationships deteriorated after raising an application. Some reported ill-feeling towards them, others direct victimisation or difficulties in finding other employment. We might hypothesise that, if applicants themselves did not experience a qualitative improvement after taking a case to a tribunal, then the chances that the tribunal will have brought wider improvements in policy and practice will be low.

Thirdly, what little research evidence there is on the consequences for employers of individual tribunal proceedings suggests that successful applications do not necessarily bring about improvements in the lot of other workers. More of Leonard's sample of applicants reported that conditions for other workers had either deteriorated or been unaffected, than reported definite gains. We should note, however, that Leonard's sample of applicants included many who would not have been in a position to assess consequent changes, since included in the sample were applicants in both recruitment and dismissal cases. A major objective of this research has been to come to a more reliable assessment of effects and consequences through case studies of organisations, and by gathering information from a wide range of informed individuals.

Fourthly, we have already noted that the tribunal process is not itself designed to bring about changes in employment practice, but to decide whether an employer has breached anti-discrimination legislation, and to provide a remedy for an offended individual. Given this background we could regard any improvements in employment practices as an added bonus.

Section 65(1) of the SDA reads as follows:

Where an industrial tribunal finds that a complaint presented to it under section 63 is well-founded the tribunal shall make such of the following as it considers just and equitable–

(a) an order declaring the rights of the complainant and the respondent in relation to the act to which the complaint relates;

(b) an order requiring the respondent to pay to the complainant compensation of an amount corresponding to any damages could have been ordered by a county court or by a sheriff court to pay to the complainant if the complaint had fallen to be dealt with under section 66;

(c) a recommendation that the respondent take within a specific period action appearing to the tribunal to be practicable for the purpose of obviating or reducing the adverse effect on the complainant of any act of discrimination to which the complaint relates.

The tribunal does therefore have the power under section 65(1)(c) of the SDA to intervene more generally in the affairs of an employer but only infrequently is the power used. It is likely that a tribunal's ability to make pertinent and apposite observations, far less arrive at well targeted recommendations, will be undermined if members of the panel are inexperienced in matters of discrimination law, or have a poor understanding of the origins of discriminatory acts. Sadly, there is evidence that such a state of affairs is the rule rather than the exception,[5] and the EOC, noting that discrimination law deals with 'subtle relationships', and that there is 'a clear need for tribunals to work towards a consistent application of the law', has recommended that there should be special training in discrimination law for panel members.[6]

Finally, to the list of factors which might indicate a limited probability of significant changes in general employment practices, we should add the lack of provision, statutory or otherwise, for systematic monitoring of an employer by the EOC consequent to a tribunal decision. It will be important for us to examine the extent to which the involvement of the EOC in assisting an applicant at a tribunal has been instrumental in effecting change. But it would be surprising if the mere involvement of the EOC at that level would be sufficient to bring about constructive developments without further interventions in the form of assistance, guidance or cajoling. Yet very little constructive follow-up of employers who have been found to be in breach of equality legislation takes place, even when the EOC has been directly involved in assisting the applicant during the proceedings, and there in consequence one would expect EOC to have discovered a lot of information about the respondent organisation.

Despite these various observations and arguments, not all commentators are pessimistic about the possibility of wider changes being brought about through the industrial tribunal process. As one commentator recently observed:

> Successful cases engender more complaints as potential applicants come to believe that using the law can provide an effective remedy. The more cases there are, the better educated the judges become and the more the law is likely to be interpreted in accordance with its underlying objectives. Therefore, the more complaints that are brought, the more likely it is that complaints will succeed. The more successful complaints and the greater the price of discriminating, the more likely it is that employers will take voluntary steps to avoid litigation by ensuring that they are complying with the law by not discriminating.[7]

Methods

This research is based on successful equal pay and sex discrimination cases occurring during the three year period 1984-86. During that period applications were successful against 108 employers and the data derives from a sample of 40 of these, that is, over one in three of the total group. It was not our intention to carry out case studies of the complete group of 108 organisations as such an exhaustive programme would not have been attainable in the time period available for the research. It was therefore necessary to restrict the size of the sample and various selection criteria were adopted.

The sample of employers is described in detail in Tables 1-4. Organisations were selected from all parts of the United Kingdom excluding Northern Ireland, and we tried to ensure that all the main types of employment discrimination, including discrimination in recruitment, promotion and transfer, and dismissal and pay were included in our case studies. Our intention was to select from the group of 108 employers a sizeable number of major private and public sector bodies. It seemed important to find out if employers with tens of thousands of employees were making changes, because the effects of any changes made would impinge on a greater number of people than changes made in small organisations. Nevertheless, small and medium-sized employers have not been excluded as it was also important to discover if organisational size was related in any way to capacity for change.

We wanted to ensure that the sample included more private than public sector organisations. We took the view that public sector employers, operating in a political arena, were more likely than private sector employers to have introduced changes, and that they therefore constituted a softer research target. In addition, there has been a greater amount of research conducted on equal opportunities policies in the public sector, especially among local authorities, and it was felt necessary to make a contribution towards redressing this imbalance. Nevertheless, private sector organisations proved much less cooperative than those in the public sector and we would like to have included more than proved willing. But, again, for comparative purposes it was necessary to have both sectors represented.

It was thought important to include case studies of organisations where the applicant had been legally assisted by the EOC especially in terms of assistance with representation. It is known that the chances of success at tribunal are significantly increased if the applicant has a representative at the tribunal who can organise, present and argue the case. We wanted to discover if legal representation was itself a factor which increased the prospects of the decision having wider impact, and, of more importance, to find out if the involvement of the EOC in the case acted as an incentive to employers to engage in a review of policy and practice.

In a very few cases brought under the SDA the tribunal makes specific recommendations to employers to examine or alter a practice or procedure which might be having a discriminatory effect. We aimed to include all cases where such formal recommendations had been issued, and, in addition, to include cases where it seemed that the attention of the tribunal had been brought to bear on particular practices or procedures but where no specific recommendation was made.

Another criterion adopted in selecting cases derived from a recognition that some cases are won only after an appeal to the Employment Appeal Tribunal (EAT) or to the Court of Appeal, and that such cases might attract a great deal more publicity than cases considered only by the industrial tribunal. We therefore wanted to find out if cases which were won or upheld on appeal were cases which had more general effects and consequences, and we therefore sought to include in the sample cases which had been heard on appeal.

Using these criteria, organisations were selected after reading all 108 industrial tribunal and EAT decisions from the three-year study period. Additional information on applicants and employers was collected from the various regional offices of the industrial tribunals, and, in some cases, from the central office of industrial tribunals.

We contacted by an introductory letter more organisations than the final forty which made up the research sample. Ten employers refused outright to participate, and all of these were private sector organisations. In fact, it would have been very easy to construct a sample of exclusively public sector bodies as these organisations presented us with very few access problems. Some employers allowed only limited access, and we had to make a judgement as to whether the information collected was of sufficiently good quality to qualify for inclusion in the sample. In some instances it clearly was not (for example, where the data amounted to only a telephone interview with a manager of a large company and where other contacts proved fruitless). In other cases, however, and especially in smaller organisations of less than 100 employees (which had no personnel structure, which were self-proprietorships, or where there was no trade union organisation), it was possible to gather exhaustive and reliable information about the organisation on the basis of more limited contact.

We have divided the research sample of 40 case studies into a primary and a secondary group on the basis of the volume and depth of information it was possible to collect in each organisation. The primary group of 20 are for the most part larger, more complex organisations with a formal line-management structure and often, but not always, with recognised trade unions. In these organisations we sought face-to-face interviews with representatives from personnel management, line management, an employee representative (generally a trade union representative or officer) and the applicant. We indicate who the interviewees were in the account of each case study. Fewer interviews were conducted in the secondary group of organisations although it was the aim to interview a management representative and, if possible, the applicant.

Interviews were conducted with a total of 102 individuals. The great majority of these were face-to-face interviews often conducted, if the interviewee was agreeable, with the aid of a tape-recorder. A few interviews were conducted by telephone. Interviews were semi-structured and were carried out using a pre-arranged question list devised for each type of respondent (management, trade unionist, applicant etc.). Although more time-consuming, data collection by semi-structured interview was judged to be preferable to data collection by a structured postal questionnaire for three reasons.

First, we were collecting often sensitive information from employers who had been found guilty of breaches of employment legislation, and information which, it was judged, might indicate continuing non-compliance with that legislation. We did not feel that information of sufficient depth and reliability could be obtained without developing a personal rapport with the interviewees. Secondly, each case arose out of a unique set of circumstances which it would have been difficult to encompass in a postal, or even fully-structured face-to-face, questionnaire. It seemed to us important to collect information about everyday workplace interactions and social dynamics in order to understand the origins of the discriminatory act and appreciate the obstacles to progressive change. This could more easily be done with the chosen methodology. Thirdly, we expected a higher rate of non-cooperation and non-response through postal questionnaires than would have been acceptable in a small population of only 108 employers.

Data collected by means of interview forms the basis of this research report, but in addition, we studied all 108 tribunal decisions, collected documentary information from employers on equal opportunity policies, and in the larger organisations collected factual data on workforce size and make-up by means of a short self-completion questionnaire.

The structure of the report
The report has four substantive chapters which consider in turn cases of discrimination in recruitment under section 6(1) of the SDA (Chapter 2), of discrimination in promotion and transfer under section 6(2)(a) of the SDA (Chapter 3) and of discrimination concerning dismissal from employment under section 6(2)(b) of the SDA (Chapter 4). Equal pay cases are considered in Chapter 5 and the conclusions of the report are presented in Chapter 6 including a tabular analysis of effects and consequences.

Within each chapter we first consider organisations in the primary group and a set of conclusions is arrived at for each employer individually. Secondary group employers are then considered followed by a summary of findings for that group. Each chapter has its own conclusions and summary which can be read separately from the text for quick access to an account of the effects and consequences of tribunal decisions for employers considered in that chapter.

All organisations have been assigned fictitious names in order to preserve the anonymity of the employers who agreed to participate and of individual interviewees. A guarantee of anonymity was, we believe, crucial in obtaining the cooperation of many employers.

Table 1   Type of employer and size in number of employees

	Sample		Group	
Type				
Private sector	28	(70%)	77	(71%)
Public sector	12	(30%)	31	(29%)
	40		108	
Size				
1-49	6	(15%)	[not known]	
50-99	3	(7.5%)		
100-499	9	(22.5%)		
500-999	4	(10%)		
1000+	19	(45%)		
	40			

Table 2   Applications and applicants

	Sample		Group	
Type				
Recruitment	8	(20%)	25	(23%)
Promotion	10	(25%)	20	(18%)
Dismissal	8	(20%)	19	(18%)
Equal pay	9	(22.5%)	25	(23%)
Other	5 *	(12.5%)	19 **	(18%)
	40		108	
Number of applicants per case				
One only	36	(90%)	96	(89%)
More than one	4	(10%)	12	(11%)
	40		108	
Total number of applicants	69		162	

*   comprised one case of victimisation, one case of 'other detriment' and three cases
      filed under more than one heading, namely, equal pay and promotion, promotion
      and victimisation, and equal pay and victimisation.

**   includes six joint cases, three cases of victimisation, nine cases of 'other detriment'
      and one case under section 12(3)(a) of the SDA.

Table 3   Region where tribunal was held

	Sample		Group	
Scotland	7	(18%)	28	(26%)
London and SE England	13	(32%)	19	(18%)
S and SW England and E Anglia	4	(10%)	13	(12%)
Midlands	4	(10%)	13	(12%)
Yorkshire and NE England	6	(15%)	16	(15%)
NW England and Wales	6	(15%)	19	(18%)
	40		108	

Table 4   Representation

Type of representation

Solicitor/barrister	26	(65%)
TU official	6	(15%)
Other	1	(2.5%)
Self-represented	7 *	(17.5%)
	40	

Legal assistance from the EOC

Yes	21	(52.5%)
No	19	(47.5%)
	40	

*   In one of these seven cases the applicant represented herself at the industrial tribunal but she was legally represented before the EAT.

In all, five cases (12.5%) were appealed to the EAT.

Notes

1. Since April 1985 statistics have been collected within the industrial tribunal system itself, and are reckoned to be more accurate than those for previous years. In addition, they are now collected on a financial rather than calendar year basis. See *Employment Gazette*, October 1987.
2. Leonard, 1986.
3. The statistics on success rates at tribunal especially for equal pay claims are subject to distortion because of an unknown number of multiple-applicant claims. Leonard has pointed out that if the figures for 1976-83 were adjusted to take account of a 630-woman case lost at a tribunal hearing, then the success rate for women applicants would be 27 per cent and not 19 per cent.
4. Leonard, 1987a.
5. Leonard, 1987b.
6. EOC, 1988, p.19.
7. Rubinstein, 1988.

2 Recruitment

The Sex Discrimination Act makes it unlawful for employers to discriminate at the point of recruitment and hiring. Discrimination can take place in the arrangements the employer makes for deciding who should be offered a job if, for example, the employer issues instructions to a recruitment agency to issue application forms to male enquirers only. In addition, there is discrimination at the point of recruitment if an employer refuses or deliberately omits to offer a person employment by, for example, refusing to consider an application due to the sex of the applicant. Finally, an offer of employment whose terms are themselves in breach of the EqPA (for example, one which offers more favourabler ates of pay to men than to women) would also be discriminatory.

In this chapter we consider eight cases where discrimination occurred at the point of recruitment. Two of the organisations are in the public sector, in this instance, local authorities, and the remaining six are private sector commercial organisations. Three primary group employers are considered first.

R1: Denton Council

Denton Council has approximately 1200 employees with over 700 of these being in blue collar occupations. The department we are primarily concerned with has less than 100 employees and the vast majority of these are in non-manual officer grades. This department houses the council's personnel function, a small unit of 5 under the day to day supervision of a personnel officer. In common with other local authorities, the council's establishments subcommittee (comprising local councillors) has a major involvement in appointments to senior posts. We describe below the procedures involved in recruiting since these are pertinent to the case.

Information for this case is derived from interviews with the following individuals: the town clerk, the personnel manager, the councillor who at the time of the tribunal chaired the establishments sub-committee and the applicant.

The tribunal's decision

The tribunal found that the council had discriminated against the applicant in the arrangements made for the purposes of determining whether she should be shortlisted, and also in failing to shortlist her for further consideration. With respect to remedy, the tribunal declared that the rights of the applicant were to have been placed on a shortlist, awarded the applicant £500 by way of compensation, and, unusually, made recommendations to the council as it is entitled to do under section 65 (1)(c) of the SDA. These recommendations were that the establishments subcommittee (a group of local councillors) should include in its membership at least one woman and that the council should set up a working party or committee to review specific aspects of the selection criteria. The applicant was legally represented at the tribunal.

Case history

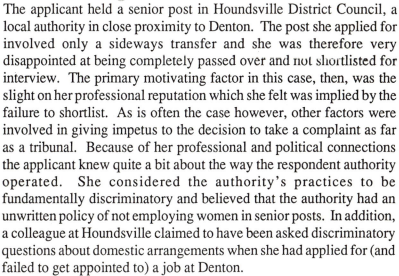

The applicant held a senior post in Houndsville District Council, a local authority in close proximity to Denton. The post she applied for involved only a sideways transfer and she was therefore very disappointed at being completely passed over and not shortlisted for interview. The primary motivating factor in this case, then, was the slight on her professional reputation which she felt was implied by the failure to shortlist. As is often the case however, other factors were involved in giving impetus to the decision to take a complaint as far as a tribunal. Because of her professional and political connections the applicant knew quite a bit about the way the respondent authority operated. She considered the authority's practices to be fundamentally discriminatory and believed that the authority had an unwritten policy of not employing women in senior posts. In addition, a colleague at Houndsville claimed to have been asked discriminatory questions about domestic arrangements when she had applied for (and failed to get appointed to) a job at Denton.

There were, it seems, two stages to the shortlisting process and since the tribunal found there to have been discrimination in both the arrangements for the shortlisting and in its outcome it is important to describe these processes in some detail. An initial sift of applications was made by the town clerk who was responsible for receiving applications and supervising the appointments process. There were in this instance 21 applications for the post and the town clerk had recommended that the establishments subcommittee, whose job it was to interview and appoint, should give particular regard, in deciding who to invite to interview, to eight applicants whom the town clerk considered were the most qualified for the job. The second stage of the shortlisting process involved a meeting of the establishments subcommittee at which eight applicants, that is, all those recommended by the town clerk, were selected for interview. The applicant was not on the shortlist.

In carrying out the initial sift the town clerk seems to have taken into consideration two points both of which he claimed justified his decision not to shortlist the applicant. First, the preferred age range for the appointment was between 35 and 40 (the applicant was 33) and suitable candidates would require to have had considerable committee experience. (The tribunal took the view that the applicant did have sufficient committee experience and noted that one of those who was shortlisted was only 32.)

The tribunal seems to have found the arrangements for shortlisting discriminatory in that these arrangements did not provide for a careful assessment of all aspects of the applicant's considerable experience. The town clerk's judgement as to her experience was in the words of the tribunal 'inaccurate'. Furthermore, at the meeting of the subcommittee which carried out the shortlist, one of the councillors present had suggested that the applicant be put on the shortlist in order to avoid any possibility that the council might be found guilty of sex discrimination. The tribunal seems to have taken the view that this intervention had provided the subcommittee with the opportunity for a more careful assessment of the applicant's qualifications which they failed to seize. Thus, although the applicant had not been deliberately omitted from the shortlist because she was a woman, a more careful assessment of her experience would have resulted in her inclusion on the shortlist. The panel took the view that the attitudes and the remarks of employees and councillors from the respondent organisation prior to and at the tribunal were indications of 'underlying discrimination against women'.

Effects and consequences

The effects of this decision can be examined at various levels, but we start with the two specific recommendations made by the tribunal. The first of these was that the establishments subcommittee should include in its membership at least one woman so that a proper assessment could be made 'of the range of factors relevant to female candidates'. It will be recalled that shortlisting was carried out by the subcommittee on the advice of the town clerk and that all members of the subcommittee were men. The recommendation of the tribunal has been acted upon and there are now two female councillors on the subcommittee. The town clerk was proud of the fact that the council had been able to go further than the tribunal's recommendation on this point. Furthermore the subcommittee's parent committee (Policy and Resources) now included three women where there had previously been none.

The second recommendation was that the council should set up a working party whose remit would be to draw up a more precise basis on which a candidate's committee work could be assessed. Such a systematic approach would, it was intended, eradicate purely subjective assessments of relevant experience. The council's officers considered this recommendation to be unrealistic and it had not been implemented. However, the council has sought to implement what it interprets as the spirit of the recommendation by drawing up a list of guidelines to govern future senior appointments of this type which is designed to spell out the nature of the committee experience required.

We can look at consequences by assessing what progress, if any, the council has made in the development of an equal opportunities policy and try to determine to what extent progress was given impetus by the tribunal's decision. There can be few local authorities who in the past few years have not had to give consideration to the issue of equality of opportunity. This makes it more difficult to pinpoint the precise effects of the tribunal decision. In Denton, as in other local authorities, officials deny that the tribunal decision prompted setting up an equal opportunities policy. However, at Denton Council progress in the development of a policy and in training initiatives was related very closely in time to the tribunal and officers' denials of a connection have to be treated with some scepticism.

A summary of the timetable of events can be given: shortlisting for the post took place in September; the applicant was informed that she had not been successful in October and raised the originating application to the tribunal at the end of November. A new personnel officer who had had previous experience of equal opportunity work in a previous local authority was appointed in February and he reported to us that work on an equal opportunities policy had already commenced prior to his appointment. In his view the policy was unconnected with the industrial tribunal decision because the tribunal had not yet taken place. The tribunal sat for four days between March and July. An equal opportunity policy had been agreed and adopted by the council by the middle of the year and at the same time the council took the decision to describe itself as an equal opportunity employer in job advertisements and council publicity material. It can be seen that practical and rapid progress was being made by the council at the time the case was going through the system but, it should be noted, before the tribunal had reached a decision on the case. We can, it seems, infer that there would have been some progress towards an equal opportunity policy even if the applicant had not been successful at tribunal.

Additional elements of the council's equal opportunity package included the issuing of a comprehensive six page Code of Practice on Advertising, Recruitment and Selection to chief officers, the revision of application forms and the setting up of a training programme on equality of opportunity for all staff involved in the recruitment process. It was estimated that this would take two years to complete.

We can also consider the influence and effects of the tribunal decision on attitudes. To what extent was the tribunal decision instrumental in changing attitudes? Was there any evidence of a genuine commitment to furthering equality of opportunity? In this case as in others, interviewees, especially those judged to have been directly involved in the discriminatory acts, often claim that the tribunal came to the wrong conclusion and at first sight it appears that attitudes may have hardened. But if the case has had any beneficial effect on attitudes and any educational effect, one might expect a recognition of the ways in which the authority's procedures and practices were at fault. In this instance, the town clerk continued to put forward the view that the two selection criteria he had used (age 35-40 and committee experience) were non-discriminatory but at the same time he agreed that there was sense in the action he was recommended to take by the tribunal and that objective guidelines made it easier to make difficult decisions. In addition the chair of the establishments subcommittee recognised that there had been problems in the past and took the view that there were 'one or two rough edges which we've polished since the tribunal'.

Conclusions

We would have to come to the conclusion that in Denton Council considerable progress had been made in developing and implementing an equal opportunity policy since the applicant raised the case. Furthermore, specific steps had been taken to implement the spirit if not the actual detail of the tribunal's recommendations. We believe that the fact that there was a tribunal at all, irrespective of its outcome, served to focus officials' minds.

Of major importance in local government is the fact that officials are accountable to politicians and personnel policies have to be justified in the political arena. Denton could at the time this case was brewing have been described as an old-style Labour council being subjected to criticism from a radical and 'younger' element within the party. The promotion of equality of opportunity was to some extent evidence of the success of this new element and cannot therefore be accounted for entirely by the tribunal case.

Interviewees commented on the publicity in the local media; the town clerk had to provide a report on the tribunal decision to the establishments subcommittee and the minutes of that meeting went to the full council. Had the decision gone in favour of the authority there would have been no specific recommendations, but it is likely that progress would still have been made towards implementing an equal opportunity policy.

There can be little doubt that in this case the panel at the tribunal demonstrated a firm grasp of sex discrimination law. In addition, the thoroughness of its analysis of the facts and its understanding of the issues involved in the case enabled it, not only to recognise wherein the discrimination lay, but also to see what steps needed to be taken to lessen the likelihood of further occurrences. In other words, the tribunal's expertise enabled it to pinpoint how discrimination might be avoided in future. Although the initial attitude of the respondent may have been begrudging, this advice was of some use to the respondent.

There is, however, the possibility of the panel overreaching itself and losing credibility with the respondent, and the second recommendation may have been an example of this. It is interesting in this respect to note that the recommendation to set up a working party found no favour with the applicant herself who regarded it as 'inadequate and missing the point'.

R2: Jones Outlets Ltd

Jones is a large high street retailing organisation with about 1000 branches throughout the UK employing in total approximately 25,000 employees of whom the majority, about 15,000, are female. In addition to a central personnel function at headquarters the company employs about 25 personnel officers based at various regional offices up and down the country. The company has six area offices and in each area there are divisional managers each of whom is responsible for about 20 branches. The branch manager has responsibility for recruiting sales staff for the branch, although in larger branches, as happened in the case we are examining, aspects of the recruitment process such as an initial sift of applications might be delegated to a departmental head within the branch. The company has its own in-house staff association of which employees are automatically members.

The branch in question employs 30 staff, of whom 13 are part-time. All part-time staff bar one are female. Of the full-time staff, there are eight sales assistants, two of whom are men, and seven departmental managers, three of whom are men. Both the manager and the deputy manager are male.

Information for this case study is derived from interviews with the organisation's personnel director at company headquarters, a branch manager , the applicant and the secretary of the staff association.

The tribunal's decision
The tribunal found that the respondent had discriminated against a male job applicant under section 6(1)(a) of the SDA, that is, in the arrangements made for the purposes of determining who should be offered employment. The applicant was awarded £150 for injury to feelings although the applicant's representative had argued for £200.

The case was supported by the EOC who provided the applicant with a solicitor. The employer was also legally represented although in previous cases (none of which according to the personnel director were sex discrimination cases) the personnel director had argued the case himself. The tribunal made no recommendations to the employer although, interestingly, the applicant recalls the chairman of the panel telling the company that it ought to improve its employment practices.

Case history

The company advertised in a local paper for a part-time sales assistant. The branch manager had placed the advertisement himself without reference to higher management, this being normal practice for such an appointment. The procedure outlined in the advertisement was that candidates were to telephone a departmental manager at the store (whom we can call Mrs Pearson) to ask for an application form. The branch manager told us that he wanted a mature person for the job so as to 'balance up the staff' in the department where the vacancy had occurred. According to the branch manager, Mrs Pearson's task was to filter out unsuitable applicants on the phone. By unsuitable the manager told us he meant candidates who were 'not mature' which meant in this instance under 25. As he told the tribunal and reiterated during the research interview, there was no instruction to consider only women for the job. The advertisement had, however, mentioned that the hours of work could be arranged to fit in with school hours and the panel formed the view that it had in fact been pitched at married women.

The manager had directed Mrs Pearson that she was to send application forms only to suitable candidates. Apparently Mrs Pearson received about 100 telephone enquiries in connection with the advertisement in the course of two days. One of the enquirers was the applicant. We were told by the manager that Mrs Pearson gained the impression from speaking to the applicant that he was only aged 18 or 19 and he was therefore told on the phone that he was unsuitable for the job. The applicant claims that he persisted in asking for an application form but was then told that the post was really for a mature woman. Mrs Pearson maintained in evidence to the tribunal that something along these lines may have been said but, if these words had been said, it was only a slip of the tongue. The tribunal took the view that Mrs Pearson had spoken to the applicant in such a way as to put him off making a formal application and the effect of this was to discriminate against him on the grounds of his sex. It took the view that a female would have been spoken to differently.

Effects and consequences

It was clear that at the local branch attitudes had hardened as a result of the case going to tribunal. The branch manager variously described the tribunal proceedings and the outcome as 'a fiasco', 'a total farce', and 'a waste of everybody's time, effort and money'. He believed the case to have been 'trumped up by the EOC to give them a job to do'. However, our interpretation was that the applicant had been so incensed by the attitude of Mrs Pearson that he would have pursued the case himself even if no assistance had been provided by the EOC. In the manager's view the applicant had pursued the case because he was unemployed and had nothing better to do.

On the surface, then, it seems that the tribunal had achieved little in changing attitudes at a local level. Nor did the manager seem to have appreciated that the applicant had no need to show that the discrimination had been intentional in order to win the case. In addition, the manager believed that the various changes in recruitment procedures that had been introduced consequent to the tribunal decision were unnecessarily laborious. The tribunal decision had clearly not brought about any commitment on the part of the company to equality of opportunity, nor, it seems, had the training in equal opportunity instituted by headquarters. There was perhaps one exception to the manager's stubborn reaction: he was able to admit that the job advertisement could have been more neutral by not mentioning school hours.

If this, then, had been a case taken against the proprietor of a small corner shop it is likely that no changes would have taken place and recruitment would have gone on much as before. It is significant, however, that no staff from headquarters appeared for the respondent at the tribunal and that apart from headquarters providing a solicitor the local branch was left to its own devices.

The branch manager reported that important changes in recruitment procedures had emanated from headquarters since the tribunal. All job applicants now got an application form automatically and no sifting was done on the telephone. There was a standard form of words used in all job advertisements and standard job advertisements had been produced for each occupational category. All job applicants received a letter from the company acknowledging the application. Corroboration of some of these changes was provided by the applicant who said that a few weeks after the tribunal he had noticed a job advertisement in the paper from the respondent company which he said looked quite different and in his view 'more professional'. Applicants were required to contact the branch manager rather than a departmental manager.

The personnel director at headquarters reported that after the case he had been required to give an account to senior management who had become concerned at losing the case. He considered that the tribunal had been such a traumatic event for Mrs Pearson that he was sure she would never make the mistake of using such a turn of phrase again. He claimed that the branch manager had been reprimanded and told to make sure that his staff were properly briefed on equal opportunity policy. However, the branch manager denied that he had been reprimanded or disciplined in any way. He took the view that the main benefit was that the incident provided a useful case study for management training.

We come up against the common problem with this organisation as with others of trying to understand developments in company equal opportunity policies from the perspective of the industrial tribunal. At Jones Outlets a formal equal opportunity policy statement was adopted by the company and issued to all branches seven months after the tribunal's finding (although it was claimed that the company had had references to equality of opportunity in recruitment guidelines and at interview briefings for four or five years). However, the personnel director maintained that the catalyst for the development of a formal policy was the Codes of Practice of the EOC and the Commission for Racial Equality (CRE) rather than the tribunal, and that the company had liaised with the CRE about the wording of the statement. The adoption of the policy was followed by a training session on the policy at company headquarters for all regional and area (but apparently not branch) managers. In addition, regular management training courses now had an equal opportunity component.

Conclusions
We formed the view that the tribunal's decision was instrumental in bringing about specific changes in recruitment methods. Most

notably, changes were made in the way job advertisements were written and in the methods of application. Telephone screening, a method which clearly allows for bias and subjective judgement of suitability, was ended. Both the branch manager and the personnel director spoke quite independently of these changes but we have not been able to ascertain to what extent they have actually been implemented in all the company's 1000 branches.

Because of the close proximity in time between the incident and the adoption of a formal equal opportunity policy and subsequent training, it is reasonable to infer that the case played a part in the formulation of this policy. However, it should be noted that the personnel director referred to the two Codes of Practice and we know that the company had been before an industrial tribunal on a few occasions with respect to the Race Relations Act (although it appears to have won these cases). As far as we know there have been no other sex discrimination cases taken against the company.

The local branch manager continued to feel aggrieved and annoyed with the tribunal's decision and no personal commitment to the development of equality of opportunity in his branch was evident. Although his attitude was hardened by the tribunal decision, the adverse effects of this were likely to have been offset by changes to procedures imposed by the organisation.

The personnel department at headquarters sought to distance itself from the discriminatory actions of the local branch. While this was a convenient evasion of responsibility, it nevertheless made it easier for the company to carry out an objective assessment from a distance of what follow-up action was necessary. In complex organisations it is not an easy task to pinpoint individual culpability or to attribute blame with a view to proposing disciplinary action against individual employees. In this case central management failed to issue clear guidelines to its branches about non-discriminatory recruitment methods until after the tribunal and the disciplining of local managers would have been inappropriate given senior management omissions and failures.

R3: Forward Enterprises Ltd

The respondent company is the proprietor of several semi-autonomous establishments involved in the communications and media industry. Unlike the previous two organisations whose branches and departments operate under the same name and present the same 'company image', the constituent establishments of this organisation go under different trading names and the general public would not necessarily know that each establishment was owned by the respondent. The company as a whole employs about 600 people but only 25 of these are based at the respondent's headquarters. The establishment where the discrimination occurred employs less than 50 people. The respondent company is in turn owned by a well-known multinational corporation which takes no interest in the day-to-day running of the company, and operational matters including personnel policy are left entirely to the respondent.

Data is derived from interviews with the personnel director, the applicant and a trade union official.

The tribunal's decision

The tribunal took the view that the applicant was discriminated against by not being considered for a reporter vacancy advertised by the company. The reason she had not been considered for the post was that she was a woman. The outcome would, in the view of the tribunal, have been the same for any woman who had applied for that particular post. The tribunal was unable to find that the applicant had been discriminated against by not being appointed to the post. The discrimination lay solely in the failure of the company to consider her.

The tribunal took into account two factors in awarding compensation in excess of £1,000. By denying the applicant the opportunity of being considered for the post of reporter, the company had, due to its monopoly position, prevented her from carrying out her profession. In addition, the degree of injury to the applicant's feelings was serious.

The applicant represented herself at the tribunal. The company employed a solicitor.

Case history

The applicant was a freelance reporter without a contract of employment at one of the respondent's constituent establishments which we can call Voxprint. It was understood by her that her employment was to be of a temporary nature and she was therefore paid at freelance rates and not as a member of staff. While she was working for the company two full-time permanent positions for reporters became vacant in areas for which the applicant regarded herself as qualified. There was considerable dispute in this case about the sequence of events, about who said what, and about what significance should be attached to any remarks made.

However, it is clear that, although the posts were formally advertised, there was no fixed method of applying for reporter vacancies. Applicants could make their interest known to the general manager or the editor at Voxprint and appointments were often made on the basis of reputation or after recommendation from one of Voxprint's sister establishments in the organisation. Interviews for posts of this type were conducted by Forward's personnel director and by Voxprint's general manager but only after suitable candidates had been selected locally at Voxprint. We gained the impression that the personnel director was there only to oversee the process and that for this type of post the decision lay with the general manager in consultation with the editor.

The selection process was therefore very informal to the extent that the person appointed to one of the vacancies had made no formal application at all and was not even interviewed. He had made known his interest only after interviews had been conducted, being appointed, it seems, because of his professional reputation.

The applicant had, however, notified her interest in writing to the general manager and also personally discussed with the editor her interest in the post. She received no formal acknowledgement of her application and was not selected for either post. Neither did she receive a letter informing her that she had not been appointed. On enquiring of the production manager why she had not been appointed she was informed that the general manager wanted to secure a balance of males and females in the establishment, and that she should not take it as a personal slight because only men had been considered for the job.

There was conflicting evidence at the tribunal from the respondent's witnesses as to whether or not only men had been considered for the vacancies but the tribunal accepted the evidence of the applicant that she had been given this reason by the production manager. The case had clearly had a considerable impact on the applicant. She could no longer continue to work for the company on a freelance basis as it had become impossible as a result of her tribunal application to maintain good relations with professional colleagues.

She had successfully managed to change careers but this had not been accomplished without considerable strain and personal difficulty. She had in any case become convinced that the company would never have employed her again if she had waited for other vacancies to crop up.

Effects and consequences

It seemed to us that there was some history of conflict between the respondent organisation and its component establishments as to who should be responsible for recruitment and appointment. It seemed that the personnel director was engaged in a process of trying, with some success, to exert authority over company recruitment methods. He had been able to use the tribunal decision as part of a strategy to gain more central control over recruitment. He believed that it was now easier for him to demonstrate to local establishments including Voxprint the benefits of central recruitment. The decision had encouraged Voxprint and others to look to the centre for support and advice on recruitment matters so as to avoid being taken to a tribunal and risk being pilloried in public.

We gained the impression that the company's response to the tribunal decision had been somewhat defensive and cynical. For instance, the personnel director said that the main lesson to be learned from the case was the need to be more careful in what was said to candidates. The one and only practical consequence of the decision had been the setting up of a half day training course in recruitment methods at each of the company's establishments.

The personnel director showed little awareness even after the tribunal of those aspects of company procedure which were discriminatory. For instance, he continued to maintain that the best people had been appointed to the two jobs and that there had therefore been no discrimination. But the tribunal indicated that the company's failure had been in not giving the applicant consideration for the job; thus the fact that others had been appointed and she had not was largely irrelevant. Furthermore, the personnel director rather perversely read the decision as an exoneration of the company's appointments procedures which he said had been given 'a clean bill of health'. He came to this conclusion because the tribunal had not explicitly said that these were discriminatory.

In the view of the personnel director the company had had the misfortune to be called to account for the attitudes of some of its managers. Attitudes were difficult to change and the real problem was that equal opportunity legislation was in advance of what most people could accept. In his view the decision had not helped to change attitudes. He believed a case such as this one had brought the legislation into disrepute among local managers, commenting that 'they all just had a good laugh about it'.

What developments there had been in the adoption of equal opportunity policies had come about because of, it seems, to unrelated pressure from the trade union which covered the organisation's professional grades. It was the union's practice to negotiate with employers for the adoption of an equal opportunity statement. Forward Enterprises had drafted a statement which had been revised by and then agreed with the union. This statement then became part of the collective agreement with the union which had been distributed to all general managers and all union representatives throughout the company. The trade union had not become involved in the applicant's case: she had allowed her union subscriptions to lapse and had not asked for any support.

Conclusions

There had clearly been no concerted effort by the organisation to learn lessons from the tribunal decision. No internal discussions at a senior level had resulted from the case. Management at Forward saw the case as an opportunity to exert control over its various establishments including Voxprint, but this was not motivated by a desire to promote equality of oppportunity and was better explained by internal political battles within the organisation. However, in consequence, it seems that local managerial discretion concerning recruitment decisions had been curtailed as senior management exerted its authority.

A joint union-management statement on equality covering some professional grades had been negotiated and the organisation referred to itself as an 'equal opportunity employer' in job advertisements. This had come about as a result of union pressure unconnected, it seems, with the case.

We find this a good example of a case where clear recommendations to an employer by the panel would have been helpful. The panel's analysis of wherein lay the discrimination remained too legalistic to be constructive. What the employer needed was a lesson in how to recruit in a non-discriminatory way. It needed to know those aspects of its recruitment practices which were likely to lay the company open to further claims of discrimination, such as the absence of application forms, job descriptions, and closing dates for applications etc. It seems to us unfortunate that an employer can go through an industrial tribunal without learning such basic points.

Other recruitment cases

In this section we analyse data collected from a further five employers in the 'secondary' group (as defined in Chapter 1) where recruitment methods have been found by the tribunal to be discriminatory. The five employers are four private sector commercial organisations and one local authority. First, we describe the main features of each case in turn and consider the impact of the decision on the employer. We then summarise the evidence on effects and consequences for the secondary group before coming in a final section to some conclusions about all eight recruitment cases.

R4: Northern Tools

The employer is a small privately owned engineering company with between 50 and 60 employees, 12 of whom are women doing secretarial or clerical jobs. None of the employees are members of trade unions. The applicant was a pupil on an engineering course at a technical college. The careers advisory service of the college was informed by the employer that it had a vacancy for a trainee machine operator and the applicant, who had completed one year of her course, was judged by her careers adviser to be a suitable candidate for the post. The careers adviser made an appointment with the production manager for the applicant to visit the factory for interview but no mention had been made on the telephone that the applicant was female. The tribunal decided that the employer was in breach of section 6(1)(c) of the SDA by not offering her employment after evidence was heard from the careers adviser that the director of the company had told her that he did not employ women on the shop floor. The respondent argued at the tribunal that the reason the applicant had not been appointed was that it had become unnecessary to take on new labour as the order for work had been taken from Northern and given to another company. However, the company failed to produce any evidence to that effect at the tribunal.

Both parties were represented at the tribunal by a solicitor and the applicant was legally assisted by the EOC. But it was the applicant's careers adviser who had been instrumental in assisting her to pursue the case from the outset. Indeed the careers service took the decision to refuse to service any further vacancies from Northern as a result of the company's refusal to employ the applicant. The employer, for his part, took the view that the careers service had been responsible for causing all the trouble and had put the applicant up to pursuing the case.

The applicant was awarded £250 by way of compensation for injury to feelings and a further £750 for what the tribunal judged to have been a lost training opportunity which had adversely affected her future career. In its written decision the tribunal stated that the applicant had not sought any recommendation and consequently no recommendation under section 65(1)(c) was made.

It was clear to us that this employer had no intention of taking any steps to promote equality of opportunity or remove job segregation. According to the general manager, women would never be allowed on the shop floor 'in my lifetime', and there was no point in his view in going through the charade of an interview if a job enquirer had no chance of employment. The main lesson to be learned from the case was not to delegate job interviewing to his departmental managers because they clearly could not be trusted to handle recruitment without getting the company into trouble. He had decided that he could not trust the careers advisory service or the job centre and so he now used a private recruitment agency with whom he claimed to have a better understanding. If there was a need to advertise then he personally took charge of screening job enquirers on the telephone so as to make sure that only appropriate people got application forms.

We had confirmation of the intransigence of the employer from the careers adviser who was shocked at the refusal of the employer to take the applicant seriously. In her view there had been no problem about the lack of female toilet facilities, as claimed by the employer. She herself had visited the premises to enquire why the applicant had been refused the job and had come to the view that it would have been suitable for the applicant to have used the facilities provided for female office staff.

The main effect of the case, then, had been that the employer had adopted recruitment procedures which more easily allowed him to discriminate against women without its becoming public knowledge.

R5: Boltons Contracts

The company provides office services on a contract basis to over 5000 business sites throughout the UK. It employs in excess of 20,000 people many of whom are part-time. The company has 70 branches each under the control of a branch manager who is typically responsible for administering about one hundred contracts and who has virtual autonomy from company headquarters in recruiting and dismissal. Regional directors are responsible for ensuring that branch managers successfully deliver the services as specified in the contract; in addition, they have a responsibility for bringing in new business. The company itself does not recognise trade unions. However, it takes the lead from its client organisations some of whom may insist that workers provided by the company join an existing trade union. Wage rates vary from one contract to another and are the subject of negotiations between the company and the client.

A branch manager of Boltons placed a vacancy with the local job centre but specified to the job centre that it wanted a woman for the job because it involved cleaning women's toilets. The job centre informed Boltons that the job could not be advertised in this way and that the company would have to consider suitable men unless there was a genuine occupational qualification for not employing men. The officer made clear to Boltons that in his view there was no genuine occupational qualification and he arranged over the telephone for an unemployed male to go along for interview. The applicant was interviewed for the job but was told that he would not be suitable and that a woman was required. The applicant returned to the job centre and was apparently informed by job centre staff of his right to take a case against Boltons to an industrial tribunal.

In its defence the company all along accepted that it had discriminated against the applicant contrary to section 6(1)(c) of the SDA but claimed that, under section 7 of the Act, there was a genuine occupational qualification which necessitated employing women only. The tribunal decided that the respondent had failed to make out a case for a genuine occupational qualification. It took the view that there was scope for reorganising the work of existing employees so that women already employed at the site could clean out the women's toilets and that the applicant could have been found alternative work in other areas of the building. The panel made no ruling on compensation and left the parties to sort out a suitable award. No recommendations were made to the employer. The company paid £200 to the applicant who was represented at the tribunal by a solicitor and legally assisted by the EOC. The employer was represented by the personnel manager.

The personnel director took the view that the case was really quite trivial and unimportant. The company's recruitment methods and selection procedures had not been the issue and the tribunal had made no comment on these. The company had admitted discriminating but it wanted the tribunal to rule on whether it had been lawful to discriminate in these circumstances. The tribunal decided the company had unlawfully discriminated, and, in the director's view, the company had tried to take note of and implement the decision. He felt, however, that the tribunal had not appreciated the employee relations problems which might ensue from transferring an employee from one job to another as such a transfer might be interpreted as a lowering of working conditions. Furthermore, if an employee was good at his or her job it was wasteful of skills and experience to transfer the employee to another job.

The company had sought to implement the decision of the tribunal by sending a copy of the decision to all branch mangers with a note outlining its implications. Apparently this was common practice with all tribunal decisions and this case was no different. Furthermore the case was used in an industrial relations course which he ran as part of the three week induction training for new managers joining the company. He thought it most unlikely that a similar episode could happen again because all managers should now be familiar with this point of law, but if it did he would be wanting to hold the manager personally responsible.

The company took the view that there was no need to have an explicit equal opportunities policy. Equality of opportunity was inherent in company policy as all jobs were open to men and women and job adverts made this clear. The fact that the company had been to an industrial tribunal should not be interpreted as a comment on the fairness of the company's procedures since the point at issue was in his view a technical matter relating to what constituted a genuine occupational qualification.

The job centre, it seemed, had encouraged the applicant to pursue the case. But instrumental in the applicant's decision to take the case had been a telephone call from Boltons branch manager who had found out about the impending tribunal case from the job centre. The applicant perceived this as a threat from the employer not to pursue the case but this only made him very annoyed and more determined to pursue it.

R6: Camley Council

The employer is a local authority which advertised a vacancy for a senior professional appointment in its administrative department. The applicant was shortlisted and interviewed for the post but failed to be appointed. The applicant's claim was not that she should have been appointed to the job, since it seems that she accepted that she had less relevant experience than the person appointed. However, she claimed under section 6(1)(a) of the SDA that the interviewing panel had discriminated in the arrangements made for the appointment by asking her discriminatory questions in the course of the interview.

While there was dispute about the precise wording of the questions allegedly put to the applicant, it seemed to the panel that some questions were designed to discover whether the applicant intended to have a family and whether this might lead her to having time off to the inconvenience of the authority. The applicant was represented by the district officer of her trade union who drew attention at the tribunal to the failure of the authority to comply with the EOC Code of Practice regarding recruitment procedures. The applicant was awarded £100 by way of compensation for injury of feelings.

The chief administrative officer was disappointed by the decision of the panel as he felt that the applicant had taken a line of questioning about family commitments out of context. Furthermore he said he had always tried to promote women to senior positions in the council, and his record and that of the council on equal opportunities had been good. However, the panel had not taken that evidence into consideration. He now accepted, however, that if the questions had been put the way the applicant alleged they were, then they probably were discriminatory. He furthermore acknowledged that he ought to have intervened as chair of the interviewing panel to stop that line of questioning. His preference was to run interviewing panels for senior posts in a more relaxed and less formal manner than might be the case for junior positions, but this might have to stop.

He believed that as a result of the case he had become more aware of the vulnerability of the authority to charges of sex discrimination and that he and his immediate staff were now unlikely to ask questions which could be construed the wrong way. There had been considerable local publicity about the case and he had made a report to the personnel committee. As a consequence he had been involved in drafting with the personnel officer for the authority a circular entitled 'Avoiding Discrimination in the Recruitment and Selection Process' which had been incorporated into a new Recruitment Manual issued to all departmental heads about 18 months after the tribunal. The relevant chapter of the manual contains a section on 'dos and don'ts' in interviewing, one of which reads, 'DON'T – ask questions relating to personal circumstances or family commitments or assume that such situations will arise in an individual's future'.

The political make-up of the council was overwhelmingly Conservative and we were told that, while the authority abided by all anti-discrimination legislation, it did not believe in subscribing to equal opportunity statements. Consequently, job adverts do not describe the authority as an equal opportunity employer. The head of administration said there was no need for the authority to go about proclaiming its practices. Evidence of the authority's commitment to equality of opportunity could be seen in its decision to circulate the EOC Guidelines for Equal Opportunity Employers to managers involved in recruitment.

R7: Foodcheck Ltd

Foodcheck is a large supermarket retailing chain with in excess of 300 branches throughout the country. Some of the largest branches employ between three and four hundred staff many of who are part-time female checkout assistants and shelf-fillers. We were told that standardisation is an important part of the company image, policy being made centrally by the company board and applied in the same way in each of the five areas.

The company was found to have been in breach of section 6(1)(a) of the SDA in the arrangements it made for carrying out the selection process for management trainees. The applicant claimed to have been asked discriminatory questions including, 'Do you plan to get married?', 'Do you plan to have a family?', and 'How do men respond to your instructions?' The company did not deny that these questions were asked but claimed that the first two questions were relevant to enquiring about the applicant's mobility and willingness to work unsocial hours. The tribunal established that none of the male candidates had been asked if they planned to start a family and that in these circumstances such a question discriminated against women candidates. The applicant was awarded £25 as compensation for injured feelings.

The applicant had been interviewed by a local branch manager and his personnel assistant after adverts had been placed in the local paper seeking management trainees. The company was engaged in a national recruitment exercise and the interview was to have been the first stage of a selection process whereby candidates were assessed for their management potential. Candidates who were successful at this stage were to go forward to a further interview at the area headquarters office. Although this was a national recruitment exercise the branch manager did not appear to have been given any definite instructions by the area office as to how the selection process should be conducted nor what qualities or characteristics he should be looking out for in candidates. The area personnel manager told us, however, that he regarded the manager as well qualified for the selection task. Nevertheless, the checklist of questions had been devised by the branch manager without reference to any higher authority, but this process was considered to be acceptable to the company.

The fact that the branch manager himself and not company headquarters had devised the questions was considered to be highly relevant by the tribunal but we found the panel's reasoning on this point to be confused. The fact that the company had not had any say in devising the questions was interpreted by the panel as an exonerating factor, whereas it seemed to us it could more properly have been interpreted as evidence of a failure of supervision. We found it difficult also to appreciate why an award for injury to feelings (£25 was the lowest award we came across in the three years studied!) should be linked to the existence of what the tribunal considered to be 'exonerating features'. The degree to which the applicant's feelings had been injured by being asked discriminatory questions seemed to us to be unaffected by whether or not the questions asked had the approval of the organisation's headquarters.

It can be argued that the tone adopted by the tribunal affects the respondent's perception of culpability and influences whether or not the respondent considers follow-up action appropriate. In this case we found very little evidence of procedural changes. For instance, there were no changes in the composition of screening interview panels; there was no specific training introduced for managers on how to carry out interviews and no attempt has been made to introduce uniformity and consistency in the selection interviews for management trainees across the country as a whole. We found this lack of uniformity noteworthy in a company which prides itself on an identifiable, national corporate image!

The area personnel manager was against providing his branch managers with a formal set of questions for screening interviews because he felt they were experienced enough to make the right decisions about candidates who had real management potential. The tribunal's decision had not made him change his mind on this matter because the applicant had in his view clearly not been of management potential in any case. He felt the tribunal had agreed with him on this point. The award had been derisory and this signified to him that the tribunal had sympathy with the company's position, although it had been required to find the company in technical breach of the Act. In his view there was no basis in the judgement for mounting a review of recruitment methods; this would have been an over-reaction considering the very mild rebuke delivered by the panel.

However, it seemed that the decision had been used as a training exercise in induction training for new managers. In addition, it had been discussed at regular meetings of area personnel directors to the extent that it was mentioned as a problem that had come up in one area. It did not seem to us that any particular effort was put into drawing out lessons or implications and we were told it was up to area personnel directors to draw whatever conclusions they felt appropriate for practices in their own area.

We were shown the company's equal opportunity policy statement (but were not permitted to retain a copy). In addition, the company training manual contained a section outlining the questions that should and should not be asked at interview. The manual is available in all branches. All employees are provided with an Employee Handbook which refers to the company's commitment to equality of opportunity.

R8: Paper Supply Company

The company is a small one-site trading organisation involved in buying and selling consignments of paper products and fancy goods. There is no manufacturing activity and the workforce consists of less than 50 employees, with men working in the warehouse and women engaged on invoicing, sales and other clerical activities. There are no trade unions and the proprietor showed considerable antipathy towards any form of workforce organisation.

The applicant saw a job advertised for a warehouse assistant for males or females at the job centre. She had had previous experience of unloading vans and lifting heavy weights and considered herself suitable and qualified. The job centre officer telephoned the respondent to arrange an interview for the applicant but was told that a female would not be suitable as the job involved lifting heavy weights and the bad language would be offensive to a woman. At the tribunal the company, represented by the proprietor, claimed that because the job required physical ability being a man was a genuine occupational qualification for the job. However, the tribunal held that the company had sexually discriminated against the woman in refusing to even consider her for the vacancy. There were in its view no grounds for a GOQ defence. The applicant was awarded £100 for injury to feelings but the panel took the view that she would have been most unlikely to have got the job had she been interviewed (no reasoning was given for arriving at this view!) and so compensation was not considered appropriate. The applicant presented her own case at the tribunal.

The proprietor told us that he had not sought at the tribunal to conceal the fact that he had discriminated against women by not employing them in the warehouse. Moreover he would continue to do so in the future because women were good in the office and men were better at lifting. It was, in his view, as simple as that and he told the panel at the tribunal that he did not think they should be allowed to interfere in his business. There was too much protective employment legislation including the SDA, and all these Acts should be abolished. The only effect of the case was that he would never again use job centres for recruiting. He now used advertisements in the local press because he could listen to job seekers on the telephone and tell them the job had been taken if he did not like the sound of them.

He did not regard the case as a defeat. The chairman of the panel had been very understanding of his predicament and he felt his honesty before the tribunal had been rewarded in that such a small amount of money had been awarded to the applicant. We find it noteworthy that an employer with such extreme views could come away from an industrial tribunal with the impression that the members of the panel had been sympathetic and understanding towards him.

Summary: Cases R4 to R8

We have found evidence of changed employment practices in two of the five cases, namely Camley Council and Boltons, but given that both of these are large decentralised organisations (especially Boltons) we wonder about the extent to which instructions issued and procedures amended will have filtered through to all sections of each organisation. Both employers sought to respond to the specific infringements which the tribunal had highlighted although neither had undertaken thorough reviews of personnel policy.

The remaining three employers showed little or no positive response to the tribunal decision. Two employers (Northern Tools and Paper Supply) proudly flouted the legislation by turning to methods of recruitment which made it easier for them to illegally discriminate, while the other (Foodcheck Ltd) made little, if any, purposive effort to change practices to ensure that its local managers would have reduced opportunities for discriminating.

Summary and conclusions

In this chapter we have considered the impact of the decision of an industrial tribunal on eight employers who have been judged to have discriminated in their recruitment practices. We have considered each of these employers in turn in order to ascertain what changes in policy and practice were appropriate, that is, to define the scope for reform, and then to find out what changes if any were actually carried out.

Because the emphasis has been on the quality and depth of change and about attitudes as well as practices, a simple headcount of organisations which have made changes may be inappropriate, but, at the risk of simplification, we can conclude that four of the eight organisations had made efforts to address the discriminatory practices found by the tribunal.

In Denton there had been considerable progress since the date of the tribunal in developing an equal opportunity policy statement and in putting this statement into practice. The panel had made recommendations to the respondent, and one of these recommendations had been fully implemented while the other had not. However, an alternative way of implementing the spirit of the recommendation had been found.

In Jones Outlets we concluded that the tribunal decision had been instrumental in bringing about specific changes in recruitment methods including the abolition of telephone screening of applicants and in the advertising of vacancies. The case played a part in the development of the company's equal opportunity policies, but other industrial tribunal race cases may also have been important as well as the EOC and CRE Codes of Practice. Attitudes had probably not been changed by the decision.

The other two employers where change was noticed were Camley Council and Boltons but in both these cases we were not able to gauge the extent to which changes would have permeated the entire organisation. Nevertheless it seemed that the specific infringements highlighted by the tribunal were attended to.

Forward Enterprises, on the other hand, had made little effort to learn lessons from the tribunal decision although headquarters had used the decision to extend its control and influence over the constituent organisations, and the semblance of a coordinated personnel function was beginning to develop. The company had recently adopted a policy statement on equality, but this had come about through trade union pressure which seemed unrelated to the tribunal decision.

No changes had been noticed in Northern Tools, Paper Supply or Foodcheck Ltd, the first two of these companies openly indicating to us that they would continue to unlawfully discriminate at their own convenience.

It is clear from the case studies presented in this chapter that employers assess the importance of the decision, and, in consequence, how seriously they are going to have to deal with the tribunal's decisions, not only by reference to the remedy proposed. Of equal importance are the messages the employer picks up from the tribunal while evidence is being led and in the written decision indicating how seriously the tribunal regards the offence. Employers gear their responses to these clues and mesages.

Although finding in favour of the applicant, some tribunal decisions appear to exonerate the employer who comes away from the hearing with the impression that the offence was merely a technical one, or even that the tribunal had some sympathy with the employer's position. If the tone adopted by the tribunal allows such an interpretation of events, it is unlikely that follow-up action will be forthcoming.

There is inconsistency in the way various tribunals consider evidence about the presence or absence of an equal opportunity policy. Some tribunals may accept the fact that the employer has an equal opportunities policy as in itself evidence of good intent and hence as an exonerating factor, whereas others may see additional culpability in the employer's failure to take that policy seriously. If the presence of a policy is to be seen as praying in the employer's aid (by and large, but not always, an unsophisticated view), then the absence of any kind of equal opportunity policy should be treated, in the same vein, as a general sign that the employer has no real commitment to promoting equality, but this interpretation is rarely arrived at. The underlying problem is that tribunals are on the whole not qualified or skilled enough to assess the value or significance of a stated commitment to equal opportunities.

3   Promotion and Transfer

Discrimination in relation to promotion and transfer is outlawed under section (6)(2)(a) of the SDA which makes it unlawful for an employer to discriminate against a woman 'in the way he affords her access to opportunities for promotion, transfer or training, or to any other benefits, facilities or services, or by refusing or deliberately omitting to afford her access to them'. In this chapter we consider eleven cases successfully brought under this section of the legislation. We examine the effects of the cases on the employment prospects of the applicant with respect to that employer as well as any wider consequences the tribunal decision may have had for the employer's policies and practices.

In promotion cases we can note that the applicant is very often a better source of information about the employer's practices than applicants in recruitment cases where contact with the employer is fleeting and could be restricted to a telephone conversation. In these cases we have therefore sought to make full use of the applicant's experience of the respondent's employment practices both before and after the tribunal. Secondly, we can note that promotion cases are more likely to arise in larger bureaucratic organisations which are hierarchically organised and have a formal career structure. This factor may go some way to accounting for the greater number of public sector organisations considered in this chapter. Of the seven public sector employers, five are local authorities (three county or equivalent upper-tier), one is a health authority and the other is a central government department. There are four private sector organisations, three being commercial companies and the other a non-profit-making charity.

P1: City Council

The employer is a local authority with about 1,000 employees and the department we are concerned with is responsible for estate management and lettings and consists of 130 staff more or less evenly divided between manual workers, such as cleaners and grounds staff, and administrative grades.

For this case study we conducted interviews with 5 people: the head of department, a section manager, a manager for the personnel and staffing department of the authority, the applicant and the solicitor who represented the applicant.

The tribunal's decision

The panel decided that the authority had discriminated against the applicant by failing to appoint her to a more senior administrative post. The panel found that even although a woman had been promoted to the post the applicant had been treated less favourably over a long period of time than a man would have been treated. Had the applicant been a man, he would, in similar circumstances, have been promoted. The tribunal found that the reasons she had been unfavourably treated over a period of time were connected with a break of service due to pregnancy, in that after she returned to the employment of the authority she had been offered work in another department which was less interesting and which had reduced her promotion prospects.

The tribunal ordered that the applicant be awarded back pay, the exact amount to be agreed between the parties within 28 days. The tribunal recommended that the applicant be appointed to a post equivalent to the grade of the post to which she had failed to be appointed within two months of the decision. Both parties were legally represented at the tribunal and the applicant was assisted by the EOC.

Case history

Before becoming pregnant, the applicant had worked continuously for the authority for a period of 12 years. She was considered to be a competent employee and had on occasions deputised for her section manager when he had been absent. Prior to going on maternity leave she had discussed with both the section and departmental manager her desire to return to work after the birth and had made a written statement of her intention to do so. The department had had no experience of women actually returning to work after maternity leave. It seems that management had not expected the applicant to return to work and had taken the view that she had intended to return only if something went wrong with the pregnancy. Her post was advertised and filled while she was on maternity leave.

The department claimed to be surprised when the applicant decided to return to work after the birth of her child. She expressed the desire to have her previous job back but was offered alternative employment at a lower clerical grade, but she was unhappy with this work even though her salary had been made up to the grade she had been on before maternity leave. The head of her department now took the view that her future lay in this new section and it was suggested to her that if she wanted to progress further she should study for a professional qualification. This she did, and the department gave her time off to go on day-release to study.

After being back at work for two years the senior administrative assistant (her previous boss) in the section she used to work in retired, and she applied for the job. She failed to get promoted and the job went to a much younger internal candidate with less experience. The applicant was very angry at the outcome and approached the secretary of the staff association who was very helpful to the applicant and suggested that she should take the case to an industrial tribunal. The applicant felt that had she not gone off on maternity leave and had she still been in her previous section she would have been promoted. She felt that the authority needed to clarify its policy on maternity leave arrangements, and that male managers had the wrong attitude to women going on maternity leave. Taking the case to the tribunal was a way of trying to get the authority to put its house in order with respect to these specific matters.

From the management's point of view the applicant had always been well treated by City Council. The department had been genuinely surprised when the applicant returned to work but had, it believed, carried out its statutory duties by providing her with work at the same rate of pay. They had tried to help her further her career by allowing her time to take professional examinations. The personnel officer at headquarters (who had experience of industrial tribunals as the employers' representative) believed the tribunal had made a wrong decision by confusing the maternity and promotion issues. He took the view that if City Council had correctly discharged its duties with regard to maternity leave (and the tribunal did not state that it had not) then there could have been no discrimination, especially as it was a woman who had in fact been promoted. We formed the view that this officer regarded the decision as the result of some kind of female conspiracy: the chair of the panel had been a woman and in his view clearly biased against City Council (although, interestingly, the applicant's solicitor also took this view); the female staff association representative was, he believed, using the affair to advance her own career and the applicant herself seemed to be fighting a battle for womankind in general.

Effects and consequences

We can look first of all at the remedy proposed and the recommendation of the tribunal. Both of these, it seems, were resolved quite quickly. The applicant was paid in the region of £1,000 and two months after the tribunal a vacancy for a senior administrative post arose in another section and it was offered to the applicant and accepted by her without being internally advertised. The applicant told us she was convinced she would not have been offered that job and would still be doing clerical work had she not taken a case to the tribunal. She expressed herself as well pleased with the new job and as a result she says she became 'charged with energy' which encouraged her to complete her professional exams.

Secondly, the case had brought about changes in the authority's practices concerning maternity leave. A circular had been issued to all departments advising that the jobs of women going on maternity leave should be kept open. The applicant corroborated that this was now standard practice. Two women, she told us, had taken maternity leave since the tribunal decision, and both their posts had been filled on a temporary basis. More generally, there had been improvements in personnel practice: all staff were now issued with a staff handbook giving details of terms and conditions of employment. Previously, pregnant women would not have known where to go to find out about maternity leave entitlements but this was now explained in the handbook.

Thirdly, it seemed that attitudes had changed: the applicant said that managers were now more cautious in personnel matters, that she herself was treated with a new respect. The departmental manager said that he was more aware of the need for a good staff appraisal system (but it was not clear to us that this had actually come about). He said that there was a need to get more women into senior positions and that they now tried to get a woman on interviewing panels.

Finally, some progress had been made towards developing a formal equal opportunities policy. The council does not refer to itself as an equal opportunity employer but it had recently adopted a policy statement. The personnel officer said the timing of this had nothing to do with the tribunal's decision although it was adopted about 18 months after the tribunal. It is interesting to note that the applicant herself became involved in the staff association's lobbying for the introduction of such a statement and helped gather together examples of policy statements from other organisations which were then put to the authority by the staff association. The elected representatives of the authority do not have party political affiliations and there had therefore been no direct political pressure for the adoption of an equal opportunity policy. In these circumstances the positive stance taken by the staff association had been highly significant and effective.

Conclusions

There seems to us no doubt that the outcome of the tribunal was a considerable shake-up in the personnel policies of City Council. The applicant is still employed by the authority and we were therefore able to have her views on changes that had taken place. For the most part she backed up the claims made by our management interviewees. She now took the view that the authority was an 'excellent' employer and claimed that there had been no bad feeling towards her since the tribunal.

The support given to the applicant by the staff association in preparing for the tribunal was considerable, as was the enthusiasm of the association in pursuing the implications of the decision. Without the support of the association and of colleagues at work the applicant might not have pursued the case and might not have continued to work for the authority after the decision. The fact that she continued in the authority's employment as a witness to subsequent changes in practice would in itself, we believe, have acted as a stimulus to the authority to get on with things.

This case might not have resulted in a decision in favour of the applicant if the chair of the panel had not played such a full role in the proceedings, as it seems she did by making what the applicant described as 'pertinent' remarks during the proceedings. She gave a lot of assistance to the applicant by way of clarifying the grounds of the application. The decision records that it had been difficult for the applicant to pinpoint the exact breaches of the legislation attributed to the respondent until the evidence had been fully heard. Another panel might have taken a much more perfunctory view of its role, and if so, the outcome might have been quite different. (There would then have been no recommendation and the applicant might not have been promoted as quickly as she was.) It was the view of the solicitor for the applicant that the chair of the panel had moved the grounds of the original application from a case of discrimination against a married woman (which sought to compare the applicant's married status with that of the single status of the person appointed to the job) to a case which sought to examine the continuing attitude of the respondent over a period of time.

P2: Carlton Council

The employer is a large upper-tier local authority with responsibility for the provision of services to around 2.5 million people. We are concerned here primarily with the authority's education department which in itself employs in excess of 40,000 people, about half of these being teaching staff. The education department has six divisions and the recruitment of teaching and ancillary staff is, for the most part, the responsibility of the department's divisional education officers under general guidelines established by the department. Divisions therefore have a high degree of operational autonomy and although there is movement across divisional boundaries, many promotions and transfers take place within the division itself.

For this case study we conducted interviews with a senior staffing officer in the education department's headquarters, a divisional education officer, the applicant, and an officer concerned with the implementation of equal opportunities for the department.

The tribunal's decision

The tribunal decided that the authority had discriminated against the applicant by not placing her on a shortlist of candidates to be interviewed for a senior teaching post. It was further decided that the authority had discriminated against her by not appointing her to the post. The applicant was awarded compensation both for injury to

feelings and for loss of earnings, amounting to in ε
No recommendations were made to the employing at.
This case was legally assisted by the EOC and bo,
represented by solicitors.

Case history

The applicant had been an assistant principal teacher for a period of 12 years and during that period had applied for seven principal teacher posts within the same division of the authority. She had on all occasions been shortlisted and interviewed except on the last occasion which was the subject of her application to the tribunal.

All the principal teacher posts in this subject were held by men, a situation unique to this division. Conversely, assistant principal teacher posts were held by women but in order not to frustrate the promotion prospects of male teachers an unofficial agreement had been reached whereby male basic grade teachers were promoted over the heads of female assistant principals to the post of principal. It appears that such arrangements had been the practice in this division for many years, and although many female teachers had brought the potentially discriminatory aspects of this practice to the attention of the authority's officers on a number of occasions, the position had continued unchanged. Although women had been considered at promotion boards none had ever been promoted to the rank of principal in this subject area.

It is important to understand the authority's selection procedures for promoted posts. Such posts were advertised in the authority's own circular (but might be advertised in other publications as well) and interested parties collected application forms from the head of their school. There were no job descriptions or specifications. Completed application forms were returned to the divisional education office and a confidential report on candidates was obtained from the candidate's head teacher. For each subject area there was an educational adviser with responsibility for ensuring that high teaching standards were maintained. The adviser gave advice to the education officer on the suitability of applicants for promotion, and typically a shortlist of applicants was drawn up by the education officer after having consulted the subject adviser.

Once a shortlist was compiled by the divisional education officer, an interview board was arranged and candidates were interviewed by

·e persons: the divisional education officer, the head teacher of the receiving school and a teacher of equivalent rank to the post advertised.

In the case in question, the applicant was not shortlisted although she had been on six previous occasions for similar posts. Her academic and teaching qualifications were excellent and she was noted as an expert in her subject area, having been on advisory panels and distinguished herself in the subject by attending in-house courses and taking part in a variety of extra-curricular activities. Over the years the applicant had become frustrated by the continual failure of the authority to recognise her talents. She had put up with these continual rejections, but was sure that her time would eventually come. This optimism was, however, balanced by an awareness of the historic failure of the authority to promote women to principal posts.

It was the failure of the authority to even shortlist the applicant which provoked her tribunal application, coupled with the fact that a male teacher in her school who was many years her junior and did not have her experience was shortlisted. In reaching its decision the tribunal drew attention to the following facts: the applicant's head teacher had sought to discourage her from applying and seemed to take the view that the post was for a man; he had provided the male candidate from her school with a better reference when the applicant was clearly better qualified than the male candidate; he had commented in his reference on aspects of her qualifications that he could not have been expected to know about and had shown favouritism towards the male candidate; the divisional adviser had asked for the applicant to be placed on the shortlist but she had been excluded by the divisional education officer; the divisional education officer had continually over a period of time refused to promote women to principal posts within that subject area.

Effects and consequences

It is perhaps not surprising that when we spoke to the education officer at headquarters he sought to distance himself from the activities of the divisional office. While this could be interpreted as an evasion of management responsibility on the part of the authority, it seemed that the tribunal had been used by the authority as an opportunity to sort out and amend aspects of personnel policy which conflicted with the authority's overall commitment to equality of opportunity. The view at headquarters was that the authority would lose the case, that there would be adverse publicity, but that the council was nevertheless quite happy to see the old-fashioned views of the division confronted as this could only have beneficial effects in the longer term.

So why did the council not settle the case prior to the tribunal and remedy matters within the division? The headquarters officer took the view that since divisional management were adamant that there had been no discrimination it was up to them to make out such a case before the tribunal. We gained the impression that sorting out the divisional office was seen as a rather delicate and difficult management task and the intervention of the tribunal made that task a lot easier. We were told that the case was not vigorously defended and that there had been no question of the authority appealing the tribunal's decision. Interestingly, the divisional officer who bore much of the brunt of the cross-examination from the tribunal (no HQ officers were called) himself took the view that the council's own solicitor had been unhelpful. He felt that she was against him during the hearing and he described her as a feminist.

However, it seemed to us that the council had permitted the situation in the division to continue over a number of years even after there had been complaints from female teachers, and had not sought to intervene. HQ officers had been able to evade any direct criticism by not attending the tribunal to explain or defend these omissions.

Yet the council had sought to use the tribunal's decision to make changes in appointments procedures. The divisional officer told us that he had been summoned by the education director and told that the applicant ought to have been shortlisted for the post. He now agreed with hindsight that it was a 'tactical mistake' not to have shortlisted her as she had been, in his view, provoked into action by her junior being shortlisted when she was not. He said that he could never accept that she should have got the post and he resented the tribunal casting a slur on his abilities to choose the best person for the post.

He confirmed that HQ had decided to take direct control over future appointments procedures for promoted posts in this subject area. As far as we could ascertain, this was an unprecedented step without parallel in other subject areas, or in any other of the authority's divisions, and it would have been seen as a clear indicator that the authority did not trust the division's ability to make non-discriminatory appointments. In the two years that had passed since the tribunal's decision there had, however, been no vacancies for principal teacher posts. (We were told that the council had a surplus of teachers and that there was a moratorium on appointments throughout the authority.) When we spoke to the applicant she was aware of a post coming up in the near future but did not seem to have knowledge of the new appointments procedures. She was therefore not confident of her eventual appointment, being convinced that the divisional education officer would continue in the future to make every attempt to ensure that she never won promotion.

The authority had also instructed changes in the composition of promotion boards within the division which had in the past inevitably been composed in this subject area only of men. (There were no female head teachers at all within the division; the divisional education officer, who had taken part in 95 per cent of promotion boards within the division, was a man and because there were no female principal teachers in this subject there could never be a female teacher of equivalent rank to judge the suitability of candidates.) The authority had therefore instructed that, in an attempt to undermine male domination of promotion panels, teachers of equivalent rank from other divisions were to be invited to sit on promotion panels in this subject area. It seemed to us, however, that the effect of this change could turn out to be fairly insignificant if getting women on to promotion panels was the objective. This was because both male and female teachers from other divisions would be entitled to sit on the panel as teachers of equivalent rank on a rota basis, and, given the distribution of men and women at principal teacher level even in other divisions, it was still likely that the third member of the panel would be male.

Another recent change, not directly connected with the decision of the tribunal, but which, in the view of the HQ officer, might have prevented the discrimination was that head teachers had been instructed to adopt a more open reporting system when compiling confidential reports on teachers for promotion panels. Head teachers had been encouraged to discuss the contents of the report with the teacher concerned so that any statement made could be challenged. Head teachers had also been advised to consult with others in compiling reports, as it had been recognised that they might not have first-hand experience of a candidate's abilities. The applicant believed that a more open reporting system would have been of major benefit to her own candidacy, as her own head teacher had at the time no in-depth knowledge of her subject area. We were told that this move had been introduced by the council as a direct result of a commitment to more openness in the way the authority conducted its business which had been made in the ruling party's election manifesto.

The applicant was critical of the progress that had been made by the council since her case and provided a good account of the continuing omissions of the council. As far as she was aware, there had been no positive attempt to learn lessons from the case. (She was unaware of the new arrangements that had been made for promotion boards, and this in itself is a comment on the failure of the council to give any publicity to these changes.) In her view the council should have been making a positive effort to encourage women to apply for promoted posts. It should have issued a statement after the tribunal expressing concern about the lack of women principal teachers and giving reassurance that steps would be taken to improve the situation. Instead there had been complete silence.

Furthermore, there should, in her view, be proper job descriptions for promoted posts and candidates should know against what criteria they were being evaluated. Notes should be kept of reasons for non-appointment and candidates should be made aware of these for career development purposes. She had been to seven promotion boards but no notes had been kept by panel members indicating how well she had performed on previous occasions. This had allowed the education officer to claim that she had not performed well at previous interviews without producing any supporting evidence. In her view the whole selection process was 'unprofessional' and too much power had been given to one individual in the divisional education office who single-handedly had been allowed to control promotions in the division for almost 20 years.

Both the council and the education department in particular now recognised that more had to be done to promote equality of opportunity. This was not the first case that the department had lost at tribunal. Promoting equality had been a major plank of the ruling party at the last election which it had won by a large majority, and in order to develop that commitment the department had set up a Working Party on Sex Equality in the education service convened by the deputy director of education and including nominees from both the authority and the teaching unions. A substantial report had been produced which examined both career opportunities for women and the content and structure of the curriculum. At the time of writing, this report had just been accepted by the full council. There was to be an equal opportunities unit set up within the department, and the chief executive's department was to make a senior appointment of an equal opportunities officer.

We tried to establish what consideration the working party had given to recent tribunal decisions in coming to its conclusions but we were told that the particularities of recent cases had not been drawn to its attention. This seemed unfortunate as lots of material of more general relevance is brought before the panel when it hears evidence.

Conclusions

It is probably inevitable that in a large bureaucracy local fiefdoms and concentrations of power develop in opposition to the centre. This was allowed to develop because of a lack of supervision by departmental headquarters. Nevertheless the department used the tribunal decision in positive ways to seek to eradicate discriminatory practices. It did this quietly and other authorities might have sought to demonstrate publicly that they were tackling discrimination. The case, it seemed, was dealt with only at officer level and we were not aware that the education committee became involved, or that its views were sought.

In parallel to the specific responses of the council to the tribunal decision, there were important developments taking place in the council's equal opportunities policies. It was clear that officers were obliged to implement the majority party's manifesto commitments and it is likely that the impetus for major changes had come from politicians and not from tribunal decisions. The decision of the tribunal in this case had confirmed officers in the view that there was room for improvement, although it is clear that some HQ officers knew that this was so before the applicant took the case.

The tribunal's decision showed considerable irritation with the authority's promotion practices and drew attention to a number of omissions and failures. Given the thoroughness of its enquiries, it would have been a simple matter for the panel to have come to some constructive conclusions about future practice by way of advice and recommendation to the council's officers. It seemed a great waste of effort to have examined under the microscope the council's promotion procedures without putting forward some helpful comments and suggestions.

Case P3: Power Supplies PLC

The respondent is a regional office of one of the principal energy supply industries in the country. It is part of a larger national corporation but in operational terms has a high degree of management independence. For instance, this particular regional office regards its equal opportunities policies as in advance of other regional offices. The employer (by which we mean the regional office) has about 10,000 employees, making it one of the biggest employers in the area. Approximately 5,500 of these are office, showroom or managerial staff and the remainder are in manual industrial grades. There are about 250 senior managerial staff.

Eighty-six per cent of industrial staff belong to trade unions with one major union predominating. There is a lesser proportion of non-manual grades, but more than 50 per cent belong to a major white-collar union. The company has a large personnel section at regional headquarters with a major responsibility for staff training and development. In addition, each of four areas within the region has an area personnel officer located out of headquarters at an area office.

For this case study we carried out a group interview with managers from the company including the personnel manager, a manpower services officer, a recruitment officer and an employee services officer. In addition, we interviewed an employee services officer about the company's equal opportunity policy and a union official.

The tribunal's decision

The tribunal found that the applicant had been discriminated against under sections 6(1)(a) and (c) of the SDA. It took the view that the arrangements made for considering candidates at interview were discriminatory in that there was no woman on the panel which interviewed the applicant. In the view of the tribunal the applicant was clearly the best candidate for the post and ought to have been appointed. The applicant was awarded £500 for injury to feelings. In addition, the tribunal made the recommmendation that the company it should review its interviewing procedures and that, when practicable, should include a woman on the interviewing panel. It also recommended that the composition of the panel should change from time to time.

Both applicant and employer were represented by solicitors. The applicant's case was legally assisted by the EOC.

Case history

The application to the tribunal was made after the applicant had failed for the second time to be appointed to the position of manager of one of the company's retail outlets. The applicant had worked with the company for some 14 years prior to the application and during that period she had gained promotion from sales assistant to deputy manager and had acted as manager of a shop during a 12 month period when the manager was absent due to illness. There had been no criticisms of the applicant's performance as acting manager and in fact she had been nominated by the sales manager for the company's Star Award in recognition of her managerial potential and motivation.

When it became clear that the manager for whom she had been deputising would not be returning to employment with the company, the post of manager was advertised and the applicant was one of the candidates interviewed. She was unsuccessful at interview and a man was appointed to the job. Five men and two women in addition to the applicant had been interviewed. After the interviews a piece of paper was found on the floor of the interview room on which had been written the words 'Good screw', and when this was investigated by the company it was discovered to have been written by one of those on the interviewing panel. From what we can understand no immediate disciplinary action was taken against the officer who had admitted writing the remark, and neither was it proven at that stage that the remark had been specifically directed against the applicant rather than against either of the two other female candidates. The applicant continued to be employed by the company at the same outlet but under the new manager appointed by the interviewing panel.

Just over a year later the job of manager at the same outlet again became vacant and the applicant once more took up the position of acting manager during the interregnum prior to the new appointment. She was interviewed again for the post of manager but a male candidate with less experience than herself was appointed. The applicant was considered by the interviewing panel to have been a good number two for the job. However, when the person appointed decided that he could not take up the job after all, rather than offer the post to the applicant, the company decided to readvertise the post. Of the two candidates, a 24 year old male and a 40 year old female, the man was appointed.

In arriving at its decision that the applicant had been discriminated against, the tribunal decided that the company demanded a higher standard of performance from female candidates. It also considered statistics on the general position of women within the company, noting in particular the fact that women comprised only 3.9 per cent of senior sales staff but 69.7 per cent of junior sales staff. It also took the view that the company had failed to carry out the general policies of equality of opportunity for women under the terms of its own equal opportunity policy which it had produced in evidence at the tribunal.

Effects and consequences

We were told that the company believed the tribunal had arrived at a wrong decision. It continued to believe that the applicant was unsuitable for the vacancies for which she had applied and that the male applicants appointed were the best qualified of the field. The company had not been persuaded otherwise by the decision of the tribunal. It believed that the applicant had pursued the case because of personal animosity towards area management and that she had a grievance against the company because her husband, also employed by the company, had been forced to leave under unfavourable circumstances.

We were told in addition that the applicant had been pushed into applying to the tribunal by an ex-employee of the company who it was again alleged had an axe to grind. We found it surprising that the company still adopted such a strong defence of its actions at the time, and we take this as evidence that official attitudes may not have changed all that much after the tribunal. The company pointed to the union's failure to back the applicant as further evidence that there had been no discrimination. The personnel manager claimed to have been told by a union official that the union would not support the applicant because she did not have a good case. When we asked a union official about the union's attitude towards the case we were told that the union could not give the applicant assistance because she was not a member but the union 'had pointed her in the direction of the EOC'. The failure to provide practical assistance did not, he claimed, imply that the union considered there to be no merit in the case.

We heard that the officer who made the sexist comments had been disciplined following the tribunal 'for bringing the company into disrepute'. The union officer thought that another officer representing the personnel department on the interview panel had also been demoted for his mishandling of the case.

The company, we were told, had not found the recommendations of the tribunal particularly helpful. In fact, it had taken legal advice on the status of the recommendations and had been advised that the company was under no legal obligation to conform to them. It objected in particular to the recommendation to include, where practicable, a woman on interviewing panels and it had not sought to implement this item.

The company took the view that the recommendations of the tribunal had been overtaken by events in that the company had begun a cooperative exercise with the EOC to examine recruitment and promotion practices and the development of equality of opportunity within the organisation. As we understand it, the joint exercise with the EOC was not prompted by the circumstances leading up to the tribunal, although both events were closely related in time. We gained the impression that the joint exercise had been highly significant for the development of equal opportunity policies within the company, but that, due to the company's belief that the tribunal had reached a wrong decision, no attempt was made to learn any specific lessons from that case. The tribunal had been 'of minor importance' and an 'unfortunate incident' which the company wanted to put behind it.

The company informed us of a number of developments in the implementation of its equal opportunity policy since the time of the tribunal. We list these developments below.

(1) The larger corporation of which the company is a part had issued a Policy Statement on Equal Opportunities to all regional companies. 1,200 senior staff from the company (that is, all 250 senior management and 1,000 staff in staff officer grades 1-7) had been invited to a half-day training course to launch the statement and to emphasise its importance.

(2) The company itself had set up 'awareness training' on equal opportunity issues and all personnel staff throughout the region had been on a two-day training programme.

much younger, he had had experience of an instructor post in a temporary capacity in the recent past. The applicant, however, took the view that her qualifications as a nurse and her broader social service experience made her a better candidate than her colleague.

The applicant took the matter up with her union representative and various meetings followed with council officials in an attempt to resolve the matter but these failed. The applicant's case rested on what she alleged one of those on the interview panel said to her when she telephoned to enquire why she had not been appointed to the post. The applicant claimed that she was told that it had been a very close thing between herself and the man appointed but that there was a need to balance the sexes at the centre. The interviewer denied at the tribunal that she had said this but the panel preferred the account of the applicant.

However, there were other aspects of the selection process which in the view of the panel led to the applicant being discriminated against. First, notes made at the interview were examined and it was found that the words 'one child' had been recorded in respect of the applicant's personal circumstances. Secondly, the panel found that the arrangements for taking up references had worked against the applicant and in favour of the male candidate and that, in the particular circumstances of this appointments panel, these arrangements had the effect of reducing the applicant's chances of success. Both candidates had provided the names of two referees as requested, the man who was eventually appointed putting down the names of two internal referees and the applicant putting down one internal and one external name. However, since it was the practice of the authority to contact only internal referees, the interviewing panel had before them two references for the male candidate but only one for the applicant. The panel therefore took the view that the person appointed was unfairly assisted by the presence of two good references.

Effects and consequences

Following negotiations between the council and the union, the applicant received £200 in compensation. Apparently the negotiations were quite protracted with the council at first being reluctant to pay any money at all and taking the view that the applicant's side should have been content with the terms of the circular described below. However, once compensation was agreed the applicant received the money quickly. She was still working for the council at the time of our interview and had been promoted to manager of a day centre. She was therefore able to speak to some of the changes that have come about since the tribunal.

The council's personnel department had issued a circular to all departmental heads after the tribunal which sought to draw out the lessons that should be learned. A copy of the tribunal's decision was enclosed with the circular and all recipient heads of department were asked to ensure that managers involved in appointments procedures were aware of its contents.

We were given a copy of this document which drew the attention of departmental heads to two items. First, interviewers were advised to take care when discussing with candidates the reasons for non-appointment. Interviewers were advised to keep a written note of any such conversations so that a record of what was said could be produced if there was any dispute.

Secondly, candidates for interview were to be better informed of what the practice was with respect to taking up references. Although the personnel unit offered no instruction to departments about best practice with regard to taking up references, departments were told that if external references were not to be taken up, then candidates should not be misled into providing them for no useful purpose. In other words, if the department's practice was only to take up internal references it should so inform applicants.

In consequence, then, the county left it up to individual departments to decide whether to accept external references. When we tried to find out about current departmental practice consequent to the tribunal the department's residential manager (who had been on the interview panel which considered the applications) said that there had been no change in practice, that is, the department continued to take up only internal references. However, the applicant understood that departmental practice had changed and that both external and internal references were now taken up as a result of new instructions issued after the tribunal. She had understood the tribunal to have made a recommendation to that effect, but there was in our view no such specific recommendation made in the written judgement. The applicant's version of current practice was confirmed by a departmental personnel officer who said that the practice was to take up both external and internal references, but we found it difficult to know how much credence to give to her version since she went on to say that this had always been departmental practice anyway (a view clearly contradicted by the facts as disclosed at the tribunal).

We formed the view that the circular issued by the central personnel department had been of limited effectiveness in drawing the attention of staff to the tribunal's decision since the residential manager said he did not know of the existence of any such circular.

There had been some progress in the development of the council's equal opportunity policies although we heard from various interviewees that these had been coming anyway prior to the tribunal. For instance, the application form had been redesigned to exclude questions about marital status and children. However, the applicant believed that her case had had something to do with the new form being introduced.

We heard too that a group of women managers had been formed within the social services department with the aim of promoting equal opportunities. This in turn had led to the officers of the council setting up an interdepartmental committee on women with representatives from each department. We were told that progress on the development of equal oportunities had been slow because of the political make-up of the council which did not regard the issue as a high priority.

Conclusions

The council never fully accepted that the decision of the tribunal had been a correct one. It took the view that the chairman of the panel had been biased against the council and that the panel had been clutching at straws by making such an issue of the practice with regard to references. The authority took the view that there was nothing inherently discriminatory about the reference procedures since the candidate with only one reference could in other circumstances have been a man.

The circular issued by the council reflected this overall view in that no attempt was made to introduce a uniform policy on references and the circular was at pains to point out that the personnel department did not believe that there had been any sex discrimination. Given the tone adopted in the circular and the discretion left to departmental managers, it is not surprising that there was confusion about what current practice now was in the social services department.

In the absence of any political initiative to promote equality of opportunity it had been left up to a group of council officers, concerned about the lack of progress the council was making, to carry the banner. The tribunal did not hear evidence on the council's equal opportunities policies and it could be argued that such evidence was not central to deciding on the question of discrimination. However, the tribunal went on to say in its judgement that the decision did not imply criticism of the council's overall policies with respect to discrimination and such a statement permitted the council to regard the application as a 'one-off' with no general implications. Remarks such as those made by the tribunal give legitimacy to policies and practices which have never been subjected to critical appraisal, and the effect of such remarks is likely to be to excuse employers from commencing any more general review of policy and practice even when it seems an appropriate course of action.

P5: Shepley Transport Company Ltd.

The employer is a privately owned bus company created consequent to the Transport Act 1985. It employs in excess of 3,000 people, but in the recent past when under the control of the local authority it was a much larger company, and 2,000 employees had been shed over a period of a few years. There is a small personnel section at headquarters consisting of a personnel director and up to three personnel officers. Each of the eight garages has a personnel clerk.

Over 90 per cent of employees are members of a major transport union which has recognised negotiating rights with the company. There are 70 female bus drivers compared with 1,100 males but there are no women at all at inspector level or in the management grades.

For this case study we interviewed the personnel officer who handled the case for the employer, the applicant and a trade union official.

The tribunal's decision

The tribunal found that the employer had discriminated against the applicant contrary to section 6(2) of the SDA by failing to offer the applicant access to the opportunity for promotion. With regard to remedy the panel made full use of section 65(1) by issuing an order declaring the applicant's entitlement to be considered for promotion, by awarding the applicant compensation by way of damages amounting to £100 and by recommending that the respondent interview the applicant for the next available promoted post and, if she failed to gain promotion, to provide her with written reasons for that failure. At the tribunal the applicant was represented by a trade union officer and the respondent by a solicitor.

Case history

The applicant was a bus driver who had made four separate attempts over a period of four years to get promotion to the rank of inspector. On the first occasion she was informed in writing by the district manager that, although she had not been appointed, she had had an exceptionally good interview and should continue to apply for future inspector vacancies.

This letter had given her a lot of encouragement about her career prospects which had led her to take up the employer's offer of a day-release course in order to improve her promotion prospects. But the employer claimed that the same encouraging letter had been sent to all unsuccessful applicants and that there had therefore been no intention to single out the applicant. The tribunal took the view that a letter couched in such terms could be misleading to recipients if candidates had not in fact had good interviews.

The applicant failed even to be shortlisted for any of three subsequent inspector vacancies and, incensed at what she considered to be senior management male chauvinism, she consulted her local union representative for advice on what to do. Apparently these initial contacts with the union were not very helpful. She considered the union branch to be in collusion with management over the allocation of senior posts. It was only when a full-time union official became involved that progress was made.

The personnel manager confirmed the prevalence of prejudice and sexist attitudes at senior levels within the company. He said the company had been doing a lot to combat racial prejudice but the issue of sex discrimination was in his view more intractable. He agreed that senior staff were inclined to favouritism and to promoting their 'mates'.

The tribunal was of the view that the applicant's experience had been as long as that of some of the men promoted to inspector posts, and furthermore that the applicant was better qualified by virtue of her course of study than some of the men shortlisted. Of greater significance in proving that there had been discrimination were written comments made against the applicant's name on a document listing the names of all the candidates for the inspector post. This document had been sent by the personnel department to two chief inspectors for their comments on the suitability of the candidates. The document was produced in evidence by the applicant and against her name one chief inspector had written 'No more women Inspectors please!!'. A second chief inspector had written, 'Another female?'. The respondent argued that these remarks were not taken into consideration when the decision not to shortlist the applicant was made, but the panel took the view that those who did the shortlisting must have been aware of the views of chief inspectors on the appointment of women inspectors.

Effects and consequences

We can first consider the applicant's situation. She remained in the employment of the company but, some three years after the tribunal, had still not progressed to inspector grade. We received conflicting reports from the applicant and the employer on whether there had been any promotion opportunities subsequent to the tribunal. It was clear that the company had been shedding labour for a number of years and it was therefore likely that there had been fewer promotion opportunities than in the past. Yet the applicant claimed that there had been one round of promotion interviews since the tribunal while she was absent on holiday. She claimed the interviews had been so timed to exclude her from consideration. We were unable to resolve these conflicting accounts. However, the applicant had received her £100 as awarded by the tribunal but she considered the amount to be an 'insult' and the personnel officer himself described it as 'derisory'.

Both the applicant and management were in agreement that disciplinary action had been taken against the two chief inpectors who had written the discriminatory remarks. The applicant said they had been 'dragged over the coals'. She was also aware that they were no longer in post and supposed that they had accepted redundancy. The personnel officer said that they had been reprimanded and prevented from having any say over future appointments.

What impact did the decision have on the development of equal opportunity policies within the company? A union official described the incident as 'a useful lesson' for the company, but according to him management 'was, and still is, dominated by white middle class males'. The tradition was that inspectors had to be men in order to deal with unruly passengers and senior management had typically been recruited from the inspector's rank. We therefore came to the view that without positive action policies which sought to train women for senior posts or which recruited women directly into senior management posts, the male stranglehold on senior positions would continue.

Management was keen to tell us about its equal opportunities policies for ethnic minorities. Monitoring of employees' ethnic background had begun about one year after the tribunal decision; statistics were kept and regularly updated on the ethnic composition of job applicants and recruits, of those promoted and those on training courses, and of those being made redundant.

There was no equal opportunity policy statement although the company claimed to have been 'concerned' to promote equality for at least ten years and it described itself as an equal opportunity employer in job adverts. This concern seemed to date from the days when the company was a department of the local authority, an authority which had a political commitment to employment equality. There was, however, no longer any direct political pressure being exerted.

Conclusions

The tribunal's recommendation that the applicant be considered at the next promotion board may well have been flouted, if we accept the applicant's version of events. For whatever reason she remained unpromoted three years later. Even if some way had been found of promoting her, a more radical solution to remedying the absence of women from responsible positions in the organisation was necessary. Neither was there any evidence of an organisational commitment to making sex equality a reality.

The company had clearly been embarrassed by the decision of the tribunal and there had been a lot of local publicity at the time which gave prominence to the discriminatory remarks of the two chief inspectors. This would have probably served as a temporary caution for others inclined to assess candidates in a similar discriminatory fashion. It seemed to be fairly widely known in the company that two chief inspectors had been disciplined (although we found it difficult to discover precisely what measures had been taken against them) and knowledge of such disciplinary action would have assisted in changing the definitions of what was acceptable management behaviour.

We concluded, however, that equality of opportunity was less of a priority than it had been in the past. When we consider that the applicant has remained at the same grade, and that she was left only £100 better off after the tribunal, it is quite difficult to argue that in this instance going to tribunal had been worthwhile.

P6: Frinkley Council

The employer is an upper-tier local authority with an education department which in itself has more than 10,000 teaching and non-teaching staff. At the time of writing the employer has a hung council with the Labour party being the largest single party. The department has a divisional structure which in common with other upper-tier authorities bears a resemblance to local authority district boundaries.

For this case study we interviewed the chief officer of the education department, an equal opportunities officer employed by the authority and the applicant.

The tribunal's decision

The authority was found guilty of three separate breaches of the SDA. It was found to have been in breach of section 6(1)(a) of the Act by failing to shortlist the applicant for a post of head teacher which it had advertised. Another application alleging discrimination for failure to shortlist in relation to a separate head teacher vacancy was rejected as it was found that another female applicant had been shortlisted. The authority was found to have been in breach of section 4(1)(d) of the Act (victimisation) on two occasions by treating the applicant less favourably in the selection process because she had made allegations that members of appointments committees regularly practised sex discrimination against female teachers. The applicant received a total of £600 by way of compensation.

The tribunal was unable to find that the applicant would have been appointed to the posts had she been shortlisted. No recommendations were made to the respondent organisation. Both respondent and applicant were represented at the tribunal by solicitors and the applicant's case was legally assisted by the EOC.

Case history

Apart from a break of about four years for child-rearing, the applicant had been in the continuous employment of the authority for about 25 years and had, prior to her period of leave, reached the position of deputy head in a large secondary school. When she returned to the employment of the authority she was again made deputy head.

The applicant had on several occasions consulted with officers of the authority as to what she ought to do to improve her promotion prospects. Officers had told her that it was more difficult for women to convince appointments panels that they were capable of running secondary schools. It had been acknowledged to her in private that appointments panels favoured men as head teachers but that she could improve her own position by taking more qualifications, and, to this end, she studied first for a Bachelor's degree and then for a Master's degree. In addition, she took several in-house courses for senior teaching staff with the intention of improving her promotion prospects and showing the authority her capabilities.

Over a seven-year period prior to her application to the tribunal, the applicant had applied for about 20 head teacher vacancies, but, with one exception, she had never been shortlisted. The instance when she was shortlisted was unusual in that she was put on the shortlist and interviewed only after writing a letter of complaint to the authority in which she pointed out that she considered the authority was discriminating against her because of her sex. Having at first been told she had not been shortlisted, she received a telephone call on the morning the interview panel was meeting inviting her for interview. Not surprisingly she did not perform well and was not appointed.

Due to her continual failure to be appointed despite her qualifications and experience in curriculum development and school management, the applicant became involved in a national group of women involved in education whose aim was to campaign on behalf of women teachers and to combat discrimination against women teachers in the educational system. The applicant took an active part in this group which received publicity at both local and national level. Her involvement in the group was known to officers of the authority.

The appointments procedure for head teachers is as follows: applications for head teacher posts are dealt with initially by the district education officer for the district in which the receiving school is sited. A Joint Appointments Committee (JAC) is convened which consists of four councillors from the education committee (including typically the chair of the education committee) and four representatives from the board of governors of the receiving school. The district education officer and an educational adviser will attend the sessions of the JAC but only in an advisory capacity, and neither will participate in decision-making. The JAC initially meets to draw up a shortlist from all the applications received and meets later to conduct interviews of the shortlisted group of candidates. The JAC is typically chaired by the councillor who is chair of the education committee.

The two vacancies which formed the subject of the applicant's complaint came therefore at the end of a long period of successive applications to the council for head teacher vacancies, none of which had resulted in appointment, and only one of which after protest had resulted in the applicant being shortlisted. In the first instance named in her application the applicant was one of 18 candidates who responded to the advertised vacancy. She was the only female. Six candidates were selected by the JAC, all of whose members were men, in a first-round procedure and this was then reduced to four who were invited for interview. The applicant was not included on the first list. The tribunal came to the view that the adviser's evidence and notes taken at the shortlist indicated that he regarded the applicant as better qualified and more experienced than the other 11 candidates rejected with her at the first stage, and equal to the four candidates selected for interview.

The second case happened within a few months of the applicant's failure to be shortlisted for the above post. On this occasion there were 54 candidates as the vacancy was also advertised outside the authority, and a number of these were female. Eight candidates were selected at a first round by the JAC. The applicant was not amongst these but one other woman was. Amongst those shortlisted was another deputy head teacher at the school where the applicant worked. The JAC were advised by the adviser and the district education officer that he should not be shortlisted since in their opinion the applicant was a better candidate. However, the JAC chose to ignore that advice.

The applicant felt she had done everything possible to further her career prospects with the authority and had taken all the advice she was given by officers as to how to improve her chances. Following this last rejection she became convinced that the authority would never appoint her because of her work with the 'women in education' group.

She further believed that the council had a long history of discrimination against women teachers of which her case was only one example. She resolved therefore to take a case to the industrial tribunal and contacted the EOC for advice and information.

Effects and consequences

The tribunal found that the applicant had been victimised by the appointments panel but we could find no evidence that any attempt had been made to discipline anyone for this victimisation. In fairness to the council, this would not have been an easy process as no evidence was produced as to who had been responsible for the applicant's exclusion from the shortlist.

The applicant took the view that her chances of promotion had not been assisted by taking on the authority at the tribunal. She was convinced that she would never be appointed head teacher although she might have succeeded in getting invited to interview panels. So much bad feeling had been caused by the case that the applicant resigned her post as deputy head teacher and pursued another career.

It seems clear that the council had treated women teachers less well than other councils over a period of years. Figures were produced at the tribunal which showed that less than 2 per cent of head teachers in mixed secondary schools in the county were women compared with a national figure of 16 per cent. Such figures indicated that women had not been reaching senior positions in the county.

The appointments procedure for head teachers is complicated and involves many different individuals including school governors, councillors and officials of the education department. The combination of individuals will change from one appointment to another. Education department officials are the only ones to provide continuity in the appointments procedure, but they largely take a back seat in decision making. School governors will have only a very infrequent opportunity to appoint a head, and, although they can exercise a great deal of power, their experience of senior appointments is therefore very limited. Although some councillors may take a special interest in educational appointments, the electoral process means that councillors come and go. These factors make it more difficult to ensure that appointments are carried out free from bias and that equal opportunity guidelines are met. In describing changes that have taken place in the authority's procedures since the tribunal, it has therefore been difficult due to the complexity of the appointments procedure to assess the extent to which the relevant weaknesses in practice have been identified and put right.

The authority's education department has been the respondent in four different complaints (including the case being considered here) to industrial tribunals since 1981. (At least three of these have been sex discrimination complaints but this case was the only one lost by the authority.) However, we were told by the chief officer that the cumulative effect of the four cases had been to 'focus minds more sharply on translating theory into practice'. He was clear that one effect of the tribunals had been purely defensive: the authority was now in a better position to reply to a tribunal application than it had been in this instance. His education officers had been informed to take a more interventionist approach by issuing a spoken reminder at shortlisting and interview panels of the obligation on the panel not to discriminate. The authority could no longer assume that all members of panels were aware of their obligations in relation to anti-discrimination legislation and they therefore had to be reminded on each occasion.

In addition, applications for promoted teaching posts were now monitored so that information on male and female candidates and appointees can be analysed. It is now the authority's policy that a note should be kept of the proceedings of the interview panel including reasons for appointment and non-appointment. However, it was made clear that the authority cannot change the procedure for appointing head teachers as these are laid down by Act of Parliament. Although the authority is ultimately responsible for decisions taken by interview panels, the ability of its officers to influence decisions is limited.

There was in the chief officer's view a major problem in ensuring that school governors acted in a non-discriminatory manner; one reason for the lack of women in senior posts was that attitudes in that part of the country were, in his view, generally more conservative.

Since the case there have been major developments in the council's equal opportunity policy, although a year prior to the case the council had already appointed a race equality adviser in the chief executive's department. Six months after the case the council adopted an equal opportunity statement, and at the same time set up an equal opportunities subcommittee. However, it was felt that the education department needed its own equal opportunities input, and a special equal opportunities subcommittee of the education committee was formed with the ability to co-opt from the wider community. The majority on this committee were women. An equal opportunity officer post was created and this officer, a woman, reports directly to the equal opportunities subcommittee of the education committee.

It seems clear that the various tribunal cases provided a stimulus to equal opportunity activity which then became self-sustaining due to a strong institutional position. Once a structure was in existence the authority began to set objectives and goals which were broader and more wide-ranging than the specific issues raised in the tribunal. The tribunal decision in the case we are concerned with here was the culmination of a longer campaign that had been fought by the applicant over several years and which served to highlight a fundamental problem of opportunity blockage for women. It seems that officers of the county had been aware that there had been a major problem but had over a period of years taken no action to tackle it. The cumulative effect of several tribunal cases had provided, along with other developments, a stimulus to action.

Were the equal opportunity measures introduced likely to eradicate the factors leading to the discriminatory actions of the appointments panel? We heard that a programme of equal opportunities training had been implemented by the education department. Most main grade teachers were appointed by head teachers without intervention by the authority and so a course entitled 'An Introduction to Equal Opportunities' had been set up for heads and deputy heads of all schools run by the authority. The course was primarily intended to raise awareness using examples and role-play.

Making progress with school governors had been a bigger problem. A pilot programme of equal opportunity training had been started but since discontinued. The course had to be arranged outside work hours and getting governors to attend had been a major problem. We heard that training for governors was going to be even more necessary under the new regulations for school governing bodies which will give lay governors exclusive rights in the appointment of head teachers. All interviewees expressed concern that the new procedures were likely to diminish the already limited ability of the education authority to ensure that no discrimination took place in the appointments process.

A statistical examination of the teachers in the authority had been conducted which showed that there was a lot of bunching of women teachers at scales one and two. The EO officer felt that women lost out on promotion opportunities due to childcare responsibilities. The absence of women as head teachers was primarily a consequence of their absence from promoted positions from which it was possible to launch a bid for head posts. (However, the present case showed that this was only part of the problem.) As a result of the statistical exercise the authority had seconded a female teacher to devise a pilot careers re-entry scheme for women which would make it easier to return after a career break. This it was hoped would help solve the supply side of the equation, that is, not enough female candidates presenting themselves for promotion. At the time of the research, the career break scheme had yet to be approved by the education committee.

The new Education Act will make the implementation of equality of opportunity more difficult as it will devolve appointments to school governors and weaken the scrutiny of the authority. The Act is likely to prove a retrograde step unless training programmes for school governors incorporate equal opportunity guidance. The ability of the authority to honour the undertakings it makes as part of the career break scheme (in essence to support the applications of teachers for service re-entry if they have attended training and undertaken 10 days supply teaching per annum during their break) will therefore be threatened by the 1986 Education Act.

We heard that the next phase of the equal opportunity programme was to introduce a new recruitment and selection programme which would include the production of detailed job descriptions and specifications for each vacancy. This would enable those involved in the selection process to match candidates to jobs in a more objective manner. It would allow selectors to assess the management skills of applicants as required for senior posts. Less emphasis need then be given to length and continuity of service, factors which generally worked against female candidates.

Conclusions

When the application to the tribunal is the culmination of a long period of unfair and discriminatory treatment as in this case, one has to look more widely than the immediate repercussions of the tribunal to find out if the causes of the treatment have been removed. The situation is further complicated by the sharing of responsibility for senior teaching appointments. Progress therefore requires that all those involved have taken steps to change attitudes and behaviour.

There was evidence that the council is now taking more seriously its remit to ensure that the selection of head teachers is carried out in an impartial manner. Specific instructions were given to education officers subsequent to the case and considerable progress had been made in the implementation of an equal opportunity policy in the education department. A plan was available for making further progress throughout the authority.

The tribunal decision resulted from a closely argued analysis running to some 33 pages of text, one of the longest and most comprehensive judgements we have seen. It seems all the more unfortunate that having made such a close scrutiny of the circumstances which gave rise to the discrimination, the tribunal was not able to sum up or draw conclusions as to how the discrimination might have been avoided. Given that the authority was found to have breached the Act on three separate counts which cumulatively had the effect of destroying the applicant's teaching career, an award of £600 seemed inadequate as recompense.

P7: Easterly Health Authority

The employer is a regional health authority (RHA) with around 6,000 staff if ambulance drivers (of whom there are about 3,000) are included. Apart from consultants, the authority does not itself directly employ medical and nursing staff; these are the employees of the region's 13 district health authorities (DHA). However, the RHA is directly responsible for the contracts of about 1,500 consultants throughout the region.

For this case study we interviewed an administrator responsible for medical staffing, a senior personnel officer and the applicant.

The tribunal's decision

The tribunal decided that the applicant had been unfairly treated by not being put on the shortlist for interviews for the appointment of a consultant. The applicant, it was judged, had been discriminated against because of her sex, but it was also found that there had been racial discrimination, the applicant being a woman of Asian origin. In her application to the tribunal the applicant had alleged sex and race discrimination in relation to her failure to obtain appointment to consultant posts on three other named occasions, but these applications did not succeed.

The tribunal decided that the question of remedy should be the subject of a separate hearing but the respondent appealed the decision of the tribunal before this took place. The respondent's appeal was dismissed by the EAT and further leave to appeal was not granted.

Both applicant and respondent were represented by counsel at the original tribunal and at the EAT.

Case history

Since coming to Britain, the applicant had held a number of senior medical posts in hospitals and, at the time of the application, she was a senior registrar. She had for a brief period held a post of locum consultant, but, despite several applications to a number of adjacent regional health authorities, had failed in all her attempts to obtain a full-time consultant position. It is important to note that, in addition to the case we are considering here, the applicant had cited another RHA as respondent in a separate application to the industrial tribunal. That application alleged racial, but not sexual, discrimination.

The applicant therefore felt that over a period of several years she had been refused employment as a consultant due to either her sex or her race or, most likely in her view, to a combination of these two factors. The applicant had undertaken a large part of her medical training abroad and it was part of her case that she believed that the medical establishment in Britain did not regard her training as of equivalent value to the training received by medical students and doctors in Britain.

Although the tribunal found that there had been discrimination in only one of the four instances cited by the applicant in the case under consideration here, the panel considered that various aspects of the appointments procedures for, and decisions made with respect to, the other three instances were relevant to its finding of discrimination in the fourth instance.

The appointments procedure for consultants is laid down by Parliament in Statutory Instrument 1982 No 276 and in an explanatory circular from the Department of Health. The regulations provide for the establishment of an Advisory Appointments Committee (AAC) which consists of nominations from the Royal Colleges, from the RHA and from the DHA. Most of the nominees are eminent medical experts, very often professors, who are nominated because of their ability to assess the qualities and expertise of candidates for consultant posts. The AAC is serviced by an administrator from the RHA (usually that person has a medical background) who is responsible for setting up and convening meetings of the AAC and who acts as chair when the committee meets.

Members of the AAC are each sent copies of all applications received for vacant consultant posts, these generally having been advertised in medical journals. Each member then selects his or her own shortlist of applicants and sends or telephones the list to the RHA. The list may or may not express a preference order, and this is left to he discretion of AAC members. The final shortlist is drawn up by the RHA and may include candidates not shortlisted by members of the AAC, or may omit candidates considered worthy of shortlist by the AAC. Shortlisted candidates are then invited to an interview before the committee. Shortlisted candidates are also offered the opportunity to visit the hospital or unit which has the vacancy with a view to finding out more about the vacant post.

On the three occasions on which the applicant was shortlisted by the RHA she was not offered the post, and although the applicant complained to the tribunal about non-appointment, as we have said, the tribunal was unable to find evidence of discrimination on either racial or sexual grounds with respect to her non-appointment in these instances. However, the tribunal noted that on the first two of these three occasions the applicant had been marked as number 2 for the posts following her interviews and that, if the candidate offered the post had not accepted, she was likely to have been offered the post instead. The tribunal formed the view that her performance at these previous interviews, if nothing else, justified her being shortlisted on the fourth occasion.

It was also considered relevant by the tribunal that various statements made by the respondent in the notice of appearance which sought to explain inter alia the reasons why the applicant was not shortlisted were untrue. For example, the notice of appearance stated that the applicant was not shortlisted because that particular vacancy attracted many more high quality candidates than other vacancies, but the panel found this not to have been the case. In addition, the notice stated that the applicant had obtained the lowest grading at the previous interviews when in fact it was clear that on two occasions she was the second choice. The respondent's case came apart at the tribunal when one of the respondent's witnesses (himself a consultant and a member of the AAC) registered disagreement with the reasons for non-shortlisting given in the respondent's notice of appearance. The notice had been written, as we understand it, by the officer of the RHA who had been responsible for drawing up the final shortlist and who had chaired the interview panel. That officer did not appear as a witness for the respondent and we gained the impression that he had been purposely excluded so as not to damage the respondent's case.

The tribunal's decision was particularly critical of the appointments procedures for consultant posts. In particular, it criticised the subjective nature of the judgements made by members of the AAC about suitability for shortlisting, and the lack of information provided by the respondent about the procedures for arriving at a final shortlist once members of the AAC had submitted their recommendations. It inferred that the respondent's inability to provide this information indicated an absence of objective criteria for selection resulting in the respondent's inability to justify why some and not others had been shortlisted.

The criticisms of the appointments procedures were accepted and added to by the EAT in its judgement dismissing the RHA's appeal. At the appeal hearing the EAT made reference to criticisms of the appointments procedure made by an industrial tribunal in a separate case the applicant had taken against another health authority. The EAT also accepted those criticisms and took the view that, even although the appointments procedure had been set up by statutory provision, it had the potential to give rise to unfair discrimination due to personal bias or prejudice.

The applicant took the view that appointments procedures for consultant posts were shrouded in secrecy. She felt that applicants being appointed to consultant posts were often less qualified and had less experience than herself, but when she had sought to enquire of the RHA as to the reasons for her non-appointment, she had suffered only a rebuff and had been accused of trying to put pressure on the RHA. She felt that AACs ought to keep written notes of reasons for appointment and non-appointment and that the RHA ought to be able to justify its shortlists. The RHA had refused to have any dialogue with her about her position and she had been forced into taking things to the tribunal in order to expose what she regarded as the shortcomings of the appointments procedures. She was sure that even if she did not win the case the publicity would force the RHA into a rethink about its procedures by bringing things out into the open.

The applicant claimed that, in a case she had taken against another RHA, where the application related solely to race discrimination, there had been elements of sex discrimination as well. She said that the opportunity afforded her to visit the receiving hospital had been turned into another interview. She had been asked why she had declined to answer questions on nationality and marital status when completing the application form for that post, and then asked about childcare and domestic arrangements. The person showing her around was oblivious to the discriminatory nature of such questioning as well as to the abuse of what was intended to be an informal visit.

The personnel officer we spoke to considered that the appointments procedure for consultant posts was controlled by senior figures in the medical profession which operated 'a network of personal connections' and handed out posts on a patronage basis. We formed the impression that lay administrators and medical officers in the RHA were at odds on the emphasis that should be given to ensuring that equality of treatment could be demonstrated in the appointments process.

Effects and consequences

The effects of this case cannot be considered in isolation from the implications of the parallel case (concerning race discrimination) which the applicant raised against another health authority (which we can call Uppertown). Many of the conclusions arrived at by the panel in that case have implications for the practices of AACs generally and there has been cross-reference between the two cases in subsequent appeals heard by the EAT. In the Uppertown case the industrial tribunal made specific recommendations which had implications for the procedure to be adopted by the RHA in making future appointments. Uppertown RHA appealed the decision to the EAT, the EAT upheld that appeal and the recommendations of the tribunal were therefore laid aside. However, the applicant was appealing against the decision of the EAT to order a fresh industrial tribunal hearing, and the outcome of that appeal was at the time of writing not yet known. If the applicant wins that appeal it would have further implications for appointments procedures in Easterly as well.

A further complication was that the applicant had not at the time of writing yet received any compensation from Easterly. The EAT in the Uppertown case found that the amount of compensation ordered by the industrial tribunal (£5,000) was excessive; this ruling has also been further appealed by the applicant. Easterly and the applicant will not be able to agree on suitable compensation until the new appeal in the Uppertown case has been heard and guidance given.

We heard of important changes in the RHA's personnel policies since the time of the tribunal. A personnel officer felt that the case itself had not prompted these changes because the authority was moving in such a direction anyway. Managers, in this case study and in others, commonly made such statements to us but we believe such statements ought to be treated with some scepticism. Managers do not like to admit that they have been goaded into action by outside agencies, and, if at all possible, would much rather be seen as the initiators of progressive changes. Within six months of the EAT decision the authority had introduced a policy statement on equality of opportunity, was describing itself in job adverts as an 'equal opportunity employer' and had set up an information system to analyse existing staff groups and job applicants by sex, ethnic origin and disability.

Job descriptions and personal specifications were now being introduced in order to 'eliminate the arbitrary, irrational and unlawful' from decision-making at appointments panels. We also heard, however, that the attempt to make the recruitment and selection process more professional had not yet been extended to medical posts, although there had been much discussion about how it could be. It was said that one problem was that AACs were governed by regulations laid down by statutory instrument and that these were therefore not within the power of RHAs to change.

That view may be only partially correct since aspects of the selection process for consultants which were criticised by the tribunals, such as the candidate's visit to the receiving hospital and the failure of the RHA to keep notes of shortlisting decisions, do not come within the ambit of parliamentary regulations but are amenable to reform by the RHA. The applicant confirmed for us that there had been no questioning of her domestic circumstances when she had applied for (and subsequently been appointed to) a consultant's job in another part of the country. Neither had that interview panel glossed over or ignored her medical experience outside Britain.

We should note as an additional effect of the tribunal decision, the view of the personnel manager that the experience of being brought before a tribunal and being asked to give account had in the main had a 'salutory effect' on the RHA; in his view, the odd adverse finding could be quite a good thing. Moreover, the tribunal's methods of operation had ensured that the motives of the individuals concerned with the case had been fully explored and cross-examined. This had, in his view, been an effective but 'most painful' way of learning lessons.

It is necessary to acknowledge the existence of other initiatives which are likely to affect the development of equality of opportunity in the National Health Service. We have not been able to establish the extent to which these wider initiatives have stemmed from industrial tribunal decisions, although it is unlikely, given the publicity surrounding this case, and the one related to it, that the tribunal decisions and the subsequent appeals would have gone unnoticed by health service managers, having, as they did, implications for the Department of Health's regulations on medical appointments. There has, for example, been the King's Fund task force on racial discrimination and the National Steering Group on Equality of Opportunity for Women in the health service.

Conclusions

Our overall assessment would be that the decision of the industrial tribunal has had the effect of adding extra pressure to demands coming from other parties for improvements in personnel procedures at least in the regions affected by the decision and more likely further afield. The decisions have helped create a climate which is more favourable to progress on equality of opportunity. However, changes are likely to be slower in coming about where powerful professional interests are involved as in the appointment of medical consultants.

The case we have been examining, when considered along with its 'sister' case, does, we believe, help to demonstrate that the final outcome of the case, that is, whether the applicant wins or loses, may not be a crucial determinant of impact, especially if a case for better equality of opportunity policies is being made out by other bodies at the same time. In the Uppertown case the applicant lost the appeal but the spotlight had already been turned on the authority's practices by the industrial tribunal. In addition, the appeal body did not seek to disagree with the observations made by the tribunal on the authority's selection process even though it disagreed with the way it had reached its conclusion. A thorough examination of the circumstances of the case which draws attention to bad practice but which results in the application being rejected may be more effective in initiating change than a decision in favour of the applicant.

Other promotion cases

We now turn to an examination of data we have collected on four promotion/transfer decisions from the secondary group of case studies. We consider the data on each employer in turn before arriving at some conclusions about the group of four as a whole. The group consists of a local authority, a department of central government, a private sector trading company and a voluntary organisation.

P8: Ford Council

The employer has a staff of approximately 8,500 of whom about two thirds are female. It is interesting to note, but not central to the case, that, as with other authorities, part-time female staff outnumbered full-time female staff by a proportion of about 3:2. The authority was taken to an industrial tribunal by a woman who had initially been employed by the authority as a part-time cleaner, but who, at the time of the complaint, had been working as acting caretaker in a centre run by the authority pending the post being advertised and filled on a permanent basis. The previous holder of the post had been a man who had retired early on grounds of ill-health. The applicant complained that the authority had discriminated against her by failing to appoint her to the post of caretaker.

The tribunal found that the applicant had been discriminated against in not being offered the job of caretaker. It took the view that she was the most qualified applicant for the job due to the fact that she had been acting caretaker for a period of some fourteen months and that there had been no complaints about her performance. No remedy was proposed at the hearing but the parties were encouraged to reach settlement, failing which there was to be another hearing to decide on remedy. The applicant was represented at the tribunal by a solicitor and the case was legally assisted by the EOC. The respondent was represented by the personnel manager.

The applicant had been interviewed for the job, along with seven other candidates, five men and two women, by a panel of three men. One of the male candidates was offered the job. In its decision on the case the tribunal noted that it preferred the evidence of the applicant to that of the respondent on a number of points where there had been a dispute as to the facts, and found evidence given by the respondent to have been unreliable and evasive. At the interview panel the applicant had been asked questions about her ability to climb ladders, questions which it was found were not asked of other candidates. In addition, she had been asked questions about her domestic arrangements. The respondent admitted in evidence that one of the reasons the applicant had not been offered the post was that it was thought her husband was ill, and that the required hours of work might conflict with her domestic arrangements.

Once all the interviews had been conducted, the applicant was called in by the interview panel and informed that the job had been given to someone else. She was told that she had been doing an excellent job but that the successful candidate had been picked because 'we want to give the boy a chance' and because they thought she would have difficulty climbing ladders.

In reaching its decision the tribunal noted that no regard had been paid by the authority to the guidance given to employers on interview procedures in the EOC Code of Practice. The applicant had never been issued with a job description; no notes were kept by the interview panel as to how the interview was conducted nor of the reasons for appointment and non-appointment; the respondent could not provide any record of the questions that had been asked at interview. Furthermore there was evidence that discriminatory questions had been asked of the applicant contrary to the Code of Practice.

We heard from the personnel manager who represented the authority at the tribunal that he had been misled by a line manager as to the reasons for non-appointment. The authority had taken the decision to defend the case believing that the applicant had been unsuitable for the job, that her performance had been poor, and that she had frequently caused offence to others by using abusive language. During the tribunal the respondent's witness changed his story completely and it became clear to the personnel manager that discriminatory questions had been asked at her interview.

There had been some important consequences folllowing from the tribunal hearing. First, it seems that the applicant and the authority were able to solve the case reasonably amicably. The line manager had been instructed to find the applicant a caretaker's job. She had been taken to several centres where there were current vacancies in order to find the one that suited her best. She was now in the employment of the authority as a caretaker.

Secondly, we were informed that the line manager and those involved in the interview had been reprimanded. In the words of the manager they had been given 'a kick up the pants'. We understood this to mean that stern words had been used but that there had been no further adverse effect on their material conditions of employment.

Thirdly, the tribunal's decision had been reported to the full council which had expressed concern about the authority losing the case and had decided that action should be taken. A fuller report on the decision had also been discussed at the establishments committee, and as a result, a memo was sent to all chief officers giving guidance on selection and interview procedures with particular emphasis on potentially discriminatory lines of questioning. We were given a copy of this memo which, without referring to the tribunal decision, covered each of the criticisms of appointments procedures made by the tribunal.

The personnel officer took the view that the decision had given him leverage to do something positive about promoting equality of opportunity. There had been important contemporaneous developments in this area, which, we heard, could be accounted for by changes in the political control of the council which had until two months before the tribunal hearing been in the control of the Conservatives. When Labour became the majority party there was a higher profile for equal opportunity policies: a policy statement was adopted; the authority began to describe itself as an 'equal opportunity employer' and copies of the EOC and CRE Codes of Practice were sent to chief officers. Labour's majority on the council was insecure and further developments (such as the appointment of an equal opportunity officer) were likely to be hotly contested.

P9: Popham Plastics Ltd

The employer is a small privately-owned company of approximately 130 employees which fabricates plastic goods. The company has two directors who are the joint owners, and who play an active role in the day-to-day management of the company. There are no trade unions. For the most part there are three types of occupation in the factory: machine operators, all of whom are men, packers, all of whom are women and fabric machinists, all or nearly all of whom are women. Each machine has to be set up to make a different type of plastic moulding and this is the job of the male machinist. A woman packer works in conjunction with the male operator removing and packing items when they come out of the machine. Tasks are in this way sex-segregated, and it has never been known for a woman to have the job of machine operator.

An industrial tribunal found the company to be in breach of section 6 (2)(a) of the SDA by failing to consider the applicant, who at the time was employed by the company as a packer, for the position of machine operator when three vacancies became available. The applicant was awarded £50 by way of compensation for injury to feelings. In a separate incident, which took place two months after the applicant had been notified that she could not be considered for the vacancy, the applicant was dismissed by the company. The applicant had also complained to the tribunal that her dismissal amounted to sex discrimination, but this part of the application was rejected by the tribunal at the same hearing. The applicant represented herself at the tribunal and the company was represented by one of its directors.

An advertisement for the vacancy had been placed, while the applicant was on holiday, and when she returned (five days afterwards) she enquired directly of the director if she could apply for the position as an internal applicant. She was told that three people had already been chosen, and the applicant alleges that she was then told that the director would not be prepared to consider a woman for any of these jobs. The jobs had been advertised as suitable vacancies for trainee operators and it was not a necessary qualification to have had experience of machine operation.

The tribunal found that the company had been inconsistent in the reasons it had variously provided for not considering the applicant for the jobs. It had been maintained that the reason was that the applicant did not have the relevant experience or mechanical aptitude, but it became clear that the company had not sought to find out what the applicant's experience was, and so could not have known whether or not she was unsuitable. It was later maintained that the applicant's enquiry had come too late and appointments had already been agreed. The tribunal therefore concluded that, bearing in mind these discrepancies in the employer's reasoning and the fact that the company did not employ women in machine operator roles, the most likely reason for not giving consideration to the applicant had been because she was a woman.

The employer gave us his view that the applicant had been a troublemaker whom it was necessary to dismiss at a later date when she refused to do a job when asked by the production supervisor. From the evidence given at the tribunal, and from what we were told at our interview with the director, it did not seem to be the case that the applicant was sacked as a direct response to her application to the tribunal. This had not been her claim at the tribunal in any case. It seemed, however, that the negative response by the company to her request for consideration as a candidate for the machine operator position, had precipitated the later incident. The director was very clear that he had been happy to get rid of her. Unfortunately we were unable to trace the applicant and so we do not have her version of events.

It was clear that there had been no changes in company procedures since the time of the tribunal. The director thought that the company had really won the case since the award had been so small and his solicitor had told him that the decision should not be taken too seriously. In the director's view tribunals had to come up with a quota of decisions in favour of applicants in order to justify their existence and he had just been one of the unlucky ones.

The decision had not commented on the company's recruitment, promotion or transfer procedures, nor had it indicated any concern about the way posts were sex-segregated. No recommendations were made. Through these omissions the tribunal had passed over an opportunity to influence clearly discriminatory selection arrangements. Given the director's view that the case had not really been lost, the only outcome of the case had been to reinforce the company view that procedures were in order, and that the episode had originated due to the applicant's bitterness against the company.

P10: Homebuild Association

The employer is a national housing association which manages about 5,000 homes and bedspaces in three main areas of fair-rented housing, sheltered housing and hostel accommodation. There are about 500 staff, with 50 of these being in the association's headquarters and the remainder located throughout the country under the control of regional managers. The association employs a varied group of professions and occupations including residential care workers, project managers, social workers, catering and domestic staff as well as clerical and administrative workers. The association has a small personnel unit at headquarters with one full-time personnel officer. That officer acts in an advisory capacity to line managers and is also responsible for pay and conditions.

The tribunal found that the applicant had been discriminated against when the association took into account the fact that she was pregnant in its reasons for not appointing her to the position of temporary warden. The applicant was awarded £250 by way of compensation, a sum which the decision notes was agreed jointly by both parties after the decision was issued. Both parties were represented by solicitors and the applicant was legally assisted by the EOC.

Following the decision, there was an appeal by the association to the EAT on the grounds that the decision seemed to be contradictory as to the precise role that the applicant's pregnancy had played in the decision not to appoint. After consideration the EAT referred the matter back to the same tribunal for clarification. When the tribunal met on the second occasion it took the view that the applicant's pregnancy had been a prime factor in the decision not to appoint her. The decision of the original tribunal in favour of the applicant remained in place.

The association runs a hostel at which the applicant worked as a senior residential worker, and, in effect, as second-in-command to the warden of the hostel. It became necessary for the regional manager to ask for the resignation of the warden of the hostel, and it was decided to appoint a temporary warden until such time as a new permanent appointment could be made. No advertising took place, and the regional manager decided (in consultation, it was claimed, with headquarters) to appoint a male colleague of the applicant as temporary warden. The applicant alleged that in a telephone conversation between herself and the regional manager, in which he explained to her how the appointment had been made, the regional manager said to her that the reason she had not been appointed was due to her pregnancy. The manager denied having made such a statement although he agreed to the tribunal that reference had been made to her pregnancy in the conversation.

The association had since appointed a new personnel officer and within 9 months of the first tribunal decision (and before the result of the appeal was known) the association had adopted an equal opportunity policy statement. We found it difficult to ascertain how the policy was being implemented. Regional and area managers enjoyed a high degree of day-to-day autonomy and recruitment remained decentralised except for jobs at headquarters where procedures came under the direct supervision of the personnel officer. The induction training programme for new employees now included guidance on the new equal opportunities policy. Existing staff had all been sent copies of the policy but no additional attempt had been made to inform and train those directly involved in the recruitment and appointment of staff.

All job adverts now indicated the association's commitment to equality of opportunity both in recruitment and in the provision of housing, and all job applicants are sent copies of the policy statement. The association had set up a staff working party to review the workings of the policy and there had been a staff conference on the subject. A new application form had been introduced which asked for information on sex, ethnic origin and disability.

We heard from the personnel officer that the tribunal had increased the organisation's awareness of the need to promote equality of opportunity. The tribunal decision had been a great embarrassment to the association and it wanted to avoid another at all costs. The association's experience of operating as an equal opportunity employer was relatively recent and in the view of the personnel officer attempts were being made to get procedures right. In her view procedures were now a lot better but there was scope for improvement.

We gained the impression that the application to the tribunal had been instrumental in raising awareness and in getting a policy set up. That policy was in need of consolidation, but the organisation's resources were limited. Of course, the existence of the policy would not in itself guarrantee that similar instances of discrimination did not occur and recruitment procedures remained for the most part decentralised. The tribunal had given no assistance to the association by way of advice or recommendation. This is unfortunate because the association would have been willing to receive advice. Nor had there, it seemed, been any follow-up action or contact from the EOC to assist policy development and implementation.

P11: Government department

The employer is the central government department responsible for the administration of prisons. The application originated from a female prison officer who claimed that her transfer to another prison as a laundry instructor was not put into effect because she was a woman. The applicant argued that had she been a male she would have secured the laundry instructor job. The tribunal found the department to have discriminated against the applicant contrary to section 6(2)(a) of the SDA by refusing her 'access to opportunities for...transfer...'. The tribunal made a declaration of the applicant's right to take up the position she had applied for, ordered the department to pay an agreed amount of compensation, and recommended that the department take action to enable the applicant to take up the position. The applicant was legally assisted by the EOC and both parties were represented by counsel.

The difficulty in appointing the applicant to the post arose from her trade union's insistence that she would only to be allowed to take up the post if she would agree not to do overtime duties. She had undertaken overtime duties as part of her contract of employment at the establishment where she was currently working. Most prison officers carried out overtime duties and it would have involved a loss of income if she had been confined to laundry instructor duties only with no opportunity for overtime permitted. However, the Prison Officers' Association (POA) refused to sanction her appointment, believing she would not be able to undertake the full range of overtime duties which male officers were expected to undertake. The POA made its objections known to the prison governor and the department wrote to the applicant saying that it could only offer her the job of laundry instructor if she agreed not to take on overtime duties. This was unacceptable to the applicant who following contact with the EOC then raised the application to the industrial tribunal.

In order to put this case in context, it is necessary to bear in mind that prison establishments are referred to under section 7(2)(d) of the SDA as establishments where being a man may be a genuine occupational qualification (GOQ) for the job. In practice this has been interpreted to mean that only male officers would be assigned to establishments with male inmates, and only female officers assigned to establishments with female inmates. The precise interpretation of the GOQ has been the subject of discussion and debate between the department and the POA over the years, and local arrangements had been worked out, particularly at establishments which had inmates of both sexes, or at establishments where female prisoners were received on remand. It should also be noted that from time to time the EOC has had discussions with the department with a view to removing rigidities which were having negative effects on the careers of women within the prison service generally.

We need to draw attention, then, to the direct involvement of the EOC in this case, not only in the sense that the Commission gave the applicant legal assistance, but also because it had taken an interest in the application of the SDA to the prison service for some time. It would be accurate, we believe, to describe this industrial tribunal case as only a part of an ongoing interest on the part of the EOC in the affairs of the department. This case is then atypical and we need to bear this in mind when considering and interpreting any effects it may have had.

Since this case was raised there has been an agreement between the department and the POA on opposite sex postings which is designed to improve opportunities for female staff to transfer to establishments previously staffed by only male officers, and vice versa. As a result, applications from both male and female discipline staff are considered for postings in any of the department's penal establishments irrespective of whether the inmate population is male or female. Officers so placed are expected to carry out a full range of duties, including overtime duties, excepting those which impinge on privacy and decency and to which a GOQ will still apply. When considering requests for transfer or promotion, applications from both sexes are considered, whereas the former procedure was to consider applications from men only for male-inmate establishments and from females only for female-inmate establishments.

In a separate case raised by a male prison officer, a tribunal had found that the operation of separate seniority lists for male and female officers with different seniority dates was discriminatory against the applicant, in that it required men to have served a longer period before they could be considered for promotion. As a consequence of this decision, and as a parallel development to the case we are considering here, common seniority lists now operate. This change has inevitably meant that promotion procedures are now lengthier and more time-consuming because the new procedures increase the numbers of staff eligible for consideration.

Officials of the department were, however, of the view that such changes were necessary and were to be welcomed. The decisions of the two tribunals had been effective in surmounting the resistance there had been to opposite sex postings. The decisions had been used in negotiations which had been taking place with the POA on these and related industrial relations matters. The cases had been useful in focusing the minds of negotiators. It was put to us that decisions of courts and tribunals carried considerable weight with the POA and that management had been able to use the decisions to pursue its goal of creating establishments which were open to both sexes.

We have considered the wider implications of industrial tribunal decisions for equality of opportunity within a government department in Chapter 5.

Summary: Cases P8-P11

We can conclude that the decision of the tribunal was effective to varying degrees with respect to three of these employers but was completely ineffective with respect to a fourth, namely Popham Plastics. At Ford Council there were at least three immediate practical consequences: the applicant was found a job, the officers were reprimanded, and a memo with guidance on interview procedures was circulated. We believe that more thorough changes should not be attributed to the decision but to changes in the political make-up of the council.

At Homebuild the case seemed to have prompted the introduction of a formal policy on equality of opportunity. However, there were indications that this was still largely a paper policy and that its penetration throughout the organisation was fairly limited. We gained the impression that the factors which got the association into trouble at the tribunal, that is, the informal nature of the promotion procedure and the lack of central supervision, had not been removed.

The case taken against the central government department was an unusual one because of the interest shown by the EOC. Leaving aside the effects of the Commission's involvement, which we believe were likely to have been considerable, the decision seems to have been used constructively by management in industrial relations negotiations, and the objections which prevented the applicant taking up the post are less likely to be made in the future.

Summary and conclusions

In this chapter we have examined industrial tribunal decisions made against eleven employers whose promotion and transfer procedures have been found to be in breach of the SDA. Five of these decisions were made against local authorities, two against other public sector bodies (a central government department and a health authority), one against a voluntary organisation and three against private sector commercial organisations. In eight of these cases applicants were provided with legal assistance by the EOC and in one other case in which the complaint was of both sex and race discrimination, the applicant was legally assisted by the CRE. Tribunals made recommendations to employers in four cases.

City Council is the case amongst this group where we can be most certain that positive changes were introduced. Such changes were likely to safeguard the jobs and protect the immediate prospects of women leaving to go on maternity leave. There had it seemed been quite a shake-up in personnel policies consequent to the case. The applicant was doing well within the organisation and she had been promoted. The case had been vigorously supported by the staff association and the applicant herself had taken an active role in subsequent efforts to promote equality of opportunity.

The case against Shepley had had a less dramatic effect. Despite the recommendation of the tribunal the applicant had not been considered for promotion to inspector, but there was a conflict between the employer and the applicant as to whether there had been any opportunities for promotion. It was clear, however, that staff numbers were declining and that in such circumstances women in general were unlikely to make it to promoted posts without positive measures being taken. It seemed that the decision of the tribunal had increased awareness of the pitfalls in current selection and promotion procedures.

Carlton Council had taken specific steps to ensure that new arrangements would govern the promotion procedures for the type of post at issue. A freeze on appointments in this subject area had, however, meant that there had been no opportunity to try out the new procedures. The applicant was still employed by the authority but had not been promoted. The authority itself had been making progress with the implementation of its equal opportunities policy and a working party had addressed the issues as they affected the education department. It is unlikely that the decision of the tribunal had of itself led to these developments.

The applicant who took the case against Surley Council had, after several unsuccessful attempts, now been promoted. The council had never fully accepted the decision of the tribunal and this was made clear in a circular sent to departmental heads. The same circular had, however, sought to give advice on procedures for taking up references but this advice appeared ambiguous, and did not seem to have reached all those involved in making selection and promotion decisions. The promotion of equal opportunities was not a priority for the council and the tribunal decision had not encouraged any wider review of practices and procedures.

At Power Supplies an officer had been disciplined as a result of the case, but, leaving this aside, the decision itself had had no direct consequences, and the company refused to accept that there had been any discrimination in the particular instance. The company had little regard for the recommendations of the tribunal and had taken legal advice on their status. The applicant had now left the company, and, although we have not discovered under what precise circumstances she left, her position in the organisation must have become difficult during and after the case. This case was unique in that the company had been involved with the EOC in a joint voluntary exercise, as a result of which there had been a radical reshaping of the company's policies on equality of opportunity. Although the company's commitment and sincerity on this issue had been seriously called into question by a union officer, the topic was clearly on the negotiating agenda and a momentum had been established.

The case against Frinkley Council resembles that against Carlton in a number of respects as it involves teacher promotion. However, in

Frinkley, the applicant left the employment of the authority worn out by her battles with the employer, and convinced that she would never win promotion. She had engaged in a long dispute with the authority which had attracted local and national publicity, and in which the authority's procedures had been criticised. Specific steps had been taken by the authority to ensure that promotion boards were aware of their responsibilities under the SDA, but aspects of the promotion process remained outside the direct control of the authority's officers, and the potential for discrimination still existed. However, it should be noted that discrimination happened in Carlton over a long period of time, even although the promotion process, unlike Frinkley, did not allow for the involvement of lay governors. As in Carlton, a far reaching review of the authority's equal opportunity policies had been undertaken, and specific steps to remedy the under-representation of women at senior teaching grades were being put into effect.

The applicant in the case against Easterly health authority had also over a period of time been rejected by promotion panels, and she had in addition taken a case against another health authority. This case was also distinctive amongst the sample because it involved both race and sex discrimination. Due to what she regarded as persistent discrimination, the applicant had given up her attempts to get jobs with Easterly, and had had to find employment in another part of the country. It was not within the scope of the authority to radically alter the appointments procedures for consultants, but the authority could have tried to interfere more than it had been doing, in order to ensure discrimination was not taking place. There was little evidence that it had sought to do so in relation to consultant appointments. However, it seemed that close scrutiny of both procedure and motive carried out by the tribunal might have a beneficial impact on the small circle of people involved in appointments procedures for consultants. Easterly has made general progress in developing an equal opportunities policy but the impetus for this was unlikely to have come from the tribunal decision.

In the four remaining cases we concluded that the decision of the tribunal had been, on balance, effective to varying degrees in three of these cases and completely ineffective in a fourth.

With a few exceptions tribunals are reluctant to arrive at conclusions, far less formal recommendations, even when an exhaustive examination of the circumstances of the case has drawn attention to clear evidence of discriminatory practices. Often what is missing is merely a summing up and a pointing to the obvious steps which an employer could take in order to remedy deficiencies in practice. Many tribunals pass over the opportunity to influence the employer when it is within their grasp to do so and even when, as in the case against Frinkley Council, the tribunal has drawn incriminating inferences from general statistical data on promotions which has been presented in evidence.

If we are right in thinking that a well argued and presented case can be of benefit in drawing the attention of the employer to practice deficiencies, and that the experience of the tribunal may be as effective in changing attitudes and behaviour as any findings or remedies proposed, it follows that even cases which the employer wins can be effective in persuading him to look again at, say, promotion procedures. This may be particularly true in cases which have gone to appeal and where the employer's practices have been subject to detailed examination on a number of occasions. Comparison of the separate cases against two health authorities suggest that the case which the applicant lost had been as useful as the case which the applicant won.

There have been further indications that constructive follow-up action by the employer is not dependent on the applicant winning the case, since there have been examples of employers reviewing practice even before the case is heard by the tribunal.

Finally, it has become apparent in this chapter that a tribunal finding against an employer is likely to be more effective if it is combined with pressure or argument from others.

Notes
1. The Equality Exchange is an organisation set up by the EOC to enable employers and training and advisory bodies to exchange information, experience and expertise on equal opportunities initiatives.

4 Dismissal

Under section (6)(2)(b) of the SDA it is unlawful for an employer to discriminate against a woman 'by dismissing her, or subjecting her to any other detriment'. In this chapter we consider eight cases of dismissal and one of detriment. Three of the cases considered here were also successful under the Employment Protection (Consolidation) Act 1978, (EP(C)A), it having been decided by the tribunal that the applicant had been unfairly dismissed. Of the eight cases, two were public sector employers and of the six employers in the private sector, two were non-profit-making charitable organisations.

D1: Dinkworth and Son Ltd

The employer supplies goods and equipment to the building and plumbing trades. It has about 25 branches throughout the country employing some 300 people in total. Dinkworth is a subsidiary of a larger holding company, which we can call A&B Holdings, and which is responsible for personnel matters and training. The branch from which the application to the tribunal was made employed 28 people at the time of the tribunal, although by the time we carried out the research this had fallen to 19. The company does not have recognition agreement with any trade unions, although at the time of the interviews about 5 of the 19 employees were members of trade unions. We learned that this was a lower proportion than at other branches.

For this case study we collected data by way of interview with the group personnel director, an area manager with responsibility for the branch and the applicant.

The decision

The tribunal found that the applicant had been unfairly dismissed by her employer. The company had acted unreasonably by failing to inform the applicant that she had the right under the company's disciplinary procedure to be represented at the interview in the course of which she was dismissed. The company had further discriminated against the applicant in contravention of section 6(2)(b) of the SDA. In dismissing the applicant the company had treated her less favourably than men who had engaged in similar types of behaviour. The parties were left to reach agreement on a financial settlement, but the tribunal ordered that any compensation be reduced by 50 per cent since the applicant had through her own actions contributed to her dismissal.

The applicant was represented by a solicitor and the company by the group personnel manager.

Case history

The applicant had been employed by the company as a clerk for almost three years prior to her dismissal. She was dismissed by the company when she returned to work after lunch having consumed alcohol to such an extent that she was unable to carry out her duties. Prior to the events leading to her dismissal the applicant had during the period of her employment been disciplined by the company for similar occurrences. The first of these occurrences took place eighteen months prior to her dismissal. The applicant had been absent from work for one and a half days and had completed the standard form used by the company giving reason for periods of absence, in which she had written that one of the reasons for absence was due to a hangover. No specific disciplinary action was taken against the applicant at that time other than the loss of one and a half days wages.

Two further incidents followed some six months later. In the first, the applicant had been drinking alcohol in a public house at lunchtime with other female employees and had failed to return to work. Along with the other women involved, she was interviewed by the manager the following day and, because, in his view, she did not have a satisfactory reason for her absence, she was sent a letter issuing her with a warning about her behaviour and alerting her to the fact that a reoccurrence would result in a final warning. In the second incident a few weeks later, the applicant failed to report for work and the following day completed an absence form giving her reason for absence as being caused by a hangover. This led to another letter from the manager issuing her with a final warning and informing her that any further incidents would result in her dismissal.

There then followed, some nine months later, the incident which led to her dismissal. That day was the applicant's birthday which she celebrated in the customary manner with other employees in the pub at lunchtime. She and her female colleagues were joined there by her own immediate manager who bought her drinks. It seemed that the occasion turned into a party with many of the works staff joining in, including several of the managers. She returned to the office, but became ill and incapable of continuing, due to having had too much to drink, and she had to take the rest of the day off.

There was by this time a new branch manager who, it seemed, was keen to establish his reputation. Having become aware of the previous warnings issued to the applicant, he decided that the time had come for some firm action and discussed the incident with the applicant's line manager. He resolved to invite the applicant for interview the next morning and this took place in the company of the line manager. According to the company's disciplinary procedure the applicant should have been informed of her right to be represented at that interview, but no such information was given and the tribunal considered this to have been unreasonable. Furthermore, the tribunal decided that the manager had failed to carry out a proper investigation into the circumstances of the incident, and if he had done so, he would have discovered that several male managers were also present at the pub, and had been responsible for getting her drunk by buying her alcoholic drinks. A second interview with the applicant took place that day and it was at this interview that the applicant was informed of her dismissal. At this interview she was informed of her right to be represented but not of her right, under the disciplinary procedure, to appeal against the company's decision to dismiss her. The tribunal found that this failure to inform amounted to unreasonable behaviour by the company, and that the dismissal was therefore unfair.

The tribunal also found that, had the applicant been a man, she would not have been dismissed by her employer. It was found that male employees including the applicant's own line manager did not have disciplinary action taken against them in similar circumstances, and that, if the branch manger had conducted a fuller investigation of the circumstances of the case, he would have found that drunkenness at work had been a fairly common occurrence.

Effects and consequences

It was clear that the whole episode had brought to light serious management problems at the company which A&B Holdings had not previously been aware of. The applicant's view was that the company had been foolish in defending the case, because many other problems were as a consequence brought out into the open. The personnel director at A&B Holdings told us that he had the applicant to thank for bringing about a review of the group's operations. Although the director was representing the company at the tribunal, he claimed only in the course of the tribunal to have found out the full story about the malpractices and slackness that had been a feature of the company's operations under different managers.

The company had been trading very badly and making a loss, but A&B Holdings had put this down to the depressed state of the local economy. Several facts came to his notice during the tribunal which led to the affairs of the company being scrutinised more closely. The regional manager was replaced and the branch manager at the company left prior to dismissal. The police were called in to investigate 'organised crime' at the company and five employees were dismissed following criminal charges, including the applicant's line manager. A new manager was now in place and the company was trading with a surplus. The director was therefore grateful that the tribunal had provided an occasion for sorting out the company's affairs.

The tribunal had also highlighted a number of failings in the company's personnel procedures which A&B Holdings sought to rectify. Although the company had a disciplinary procedure, it was clear that very few employees were aware of its existence. Instructions were given that all employees were to be made aware of grievance procedures and a copy of the code was to be placed on company notice boards and issued to all employees. The case was discussed at a meeting of regional managers and instructions were issued to regional managers to communicate to branch managers that no one was to be dismissed without reference upwards first. If there was some urgency, an employee was to be suspended pending further enquiries.

The applicant was asked by the tribunal if she wanted her job back but she told the panel that life would be very tough for her if she returned. A figure of £5,000 was agreed between her solicitor and the company and this was reduced by 50 per cent due to the tribunal's finding that her behaviour had contributed to her dismissal. The applicant believed that she had been cheated of £700 by the company, receiving in the end only £1,700. The company acknowledged to us that her solicitor had made an error in the calculations, but that it was not up to the company to draw this to the other party's attention.

The applicant told us that it was part of the agreement with the company that the company would provide her with a job reference. Her concern was that she would never be able to get another job if she had a record of drunkenness from a previous employer. She said the company had complied with its agreement and no mention of the dismissal was made in the reference provided. However, at the time of our interview (some two years after the dismissal) the applicant had not yet managed to obtain another job.

There was no evidence that the company had embarked on any wider review of personnel policies. Nor had it sought to give a higher profile to its equal opportunity policy statement which consisted of a few lines in the staff handbook ('to develop the full potential of all employees...with no discrimination against sex, race, colour or creed'). The director had had some previous experience of tribunals. A few years prior to the present case the company had lost an equal pay claim at another branch. He claimed the loss of the case led to a visit from an EOC officer, but there had been no longer-term consequences, and the officer had seemed content with his assertion that it had been a one-off case.

Conclusions

The case had precipitated a wide-ranging investigation into the affairs of the company by the group personnel department. The police had been called in, a number of employees were dismissed and the company had been set on a more profitable footing. None of these developments would, however, of themselves have ensured future compliance with anti-discrimination legislation, although, as a result, dismissal procedures were tightened up and knowledge of the company's grievance procedure became more widespread.

The applicant did not want her job back but she felt she had been cheated out of some of the compensation to which she had been entitled. She had not found alternative employment.

The company had an undeveloped equal opportunity policy which the director admitted had been included in the staff conditions of service handbook without thought to implementation. The case itself had not prompted any wider review of that policy.

D2: Woodgate Area Courts Committee

The Woodgate Area Courts Committee provides a court clerk and administrative service to a group of local magistrates courts. The case we are concerned with arose at one of the courts in the Woodgate group. Due to a reorganisation of local government since the time of the tribunal, the courts committee has been reconstituted into various smaller courts committees serving one local court only. Although the respondent at the tribunal was the (now abolished) committee named above, for the purposes of the case study we concentrate on its replacement which we can call the Dalton Courts Committee. This is where the applicant would now be working, had she not been dismissed by the committee and had she chosen to stay with her employer.

Dalton Court employs 30 staff excluding the magistrates (who technically are not employees of the court). There is a professional court clerk staff of eight including the Clerk to the Justices and the remaining staff are administrative, being employed in, for example, the scheduling of cases, the collection of fines and court usher duties.

For this case study we interviewed the Clerk to the Justices at Dalton, the applicant and her legal representative.

The decision

The applicant claimed that she had been dismissed by her employer due to the fact that she had become pregnant and claimed that this amounted to sex discrimination. An industrial tribunal found that the employer had not discriminated but the applicant appealed to the EAT. The EAT referred the case to a newly constituted tribunal for a re-hearing and that tribunal ruled that the applicant had been discriminated against in being dismissed by the courts committee. The tribunal left the parties to agree compensation. Although the tribunal did not order the reinstatement of the applicant, nor was any formal recommendation made, the tribunal expressed the hope that the committee would re-employ the applicant if a suitable vacancy occurred.

For her appeal to the EAT the applicant was legally assisted by the EOC. She was legally represented throughout all the hearings as was the courts committee.

Case history

A courts committee is typically appointed annually at a general meeting of all magistrates attached to a particular court (or, in the case of Woodgate, a particular group of courts). Its function is to act as a kind of staffing, personnel and house committee and to ensure the smooth functioning of court business. One of its tasks is to appoint all court clerk staff and in this task it sits with the Clerk to the Justices who is, so to speak, the head clerk. Administrative staff will normally be appointed by the clerk alone, but with account given to the courts committee.

The applicant was appointed by the Woodgate Area Courts Committee to work as a trainee court clerk at the Dalton Court. The applicant was a recent law graduate and the training period for court clerks who were graduates was two years, but it was often possible for astute trainees to complete the training in one year only. It was likely that the applicant, had she stayed, would have completed in one year. Appointment of trainees involved a six-month probationary period.

The applicant had been employed for only six weeks when she discovered she was pregnant. She applied to the courts committee for four months leave to cover a period before and after the birth. She did not intend to take this leave immediately, and by the time she went off on leave she would have completed seven months of what had now become a 12-month training period. The committee refused her request for leave and terminated her employment taking the view that becoming pregnant during the training period was a frustration of her contract. The applicant was allowed to make an appeal to a special meeting of the courts committee, but her appeal was refused and because she was still on probation, she was not permitted to use the courts committee's grievance procedure.

At the second tribunal the employer agreed that the applicant had been dismissed by reason of her pregnancy. It justified the failure to grant the applicant leave to have her baby on the same grounds that it would have refused, and in the past had refused, a request from a male employee for extended unpaid leave to visit a relative abroad. The employer also claimed that it would have treated a male employee who had to have four and a half months off for a complicated operation in the same way by dismissing him. It therefore denied sex discrimination. However, the tribunal took the view that discrimination against motherhood, including mothers-to-be, amounted to sex discrimination and since the employer had produced no evidence to show that it had acted similarly by dismissing a male who required a similar period of absence due to illness, the action in dismissing the applicant amounted in this case to sex discrimination.

Effects and consequences

The applicant received £1,200 in compensation. Because the EOC decided not to provide the applicant with legal assistance once the appeal had been won at the EAT, she had herself to find money to pay for a barrister at the second tribunal hearing. This she managed to do by borrowing money which had in the end to be paid back from the compensation received. The applicant felt aggrieved at being dropped by the EOC, once it had succeeded in getting a legal point proved at the EAT.

Despite the tribunal's hope that the applicant would get her job back at the court the applicant had no intention of, as she put it, 'demeaning herself' by reapplying. She had by this time changed careers in a direction which offered the possibility of part-time work, enabling her to have time to look after her child.

The case seems to have only confirmed the court clerk in his reservations concerning the appointment of women staff. He told us it was his view that men made better court clerks because they could cope much better with a broader range of cases than women, who, he considered, tended to become emotionally involved in a case. Women were alright for some cases where a conciliatory approach might be appropriate. He was therefore always faced with the problem of asking himself whether a female court clerk was suitable for a case. This sort of dilemma did not arise with respect to male court clerks.

The case had in his view shown up the difficulties of appointing female staff of child-bearing age. The court was taking a great risk by appointing such women because it meant temporary staff had to be appointed while they were off on maternity leave, and this often resulted in the work not being done properly. In his view, the best way to avoid a recurrence of this type of case would be for him to enquire at the appointments interview into how the applicant saw her career with the court developing, and to discuss with the applicant her personal circumstances in order to find out if marriage was a possibility. There was no awareness on his part that such questions could themselves be found to be discriminatory.

In his view it was very unlikely that the courts committee would ever make the mistake again of dismissing an employee on grounds of pregnancy. It could, if it so wished, decide to do so, but it would be up to him as clerk to advise the committee of the implications of such a course of action in the light of the tribunal's decision.

The case had had no wider implications. There were no changes in appointments procedures, nor in how dismissal decisions were taken. While the case was in progress the Woodgate courts committee was abolished, and there was therefore no opportunity even to consider the implications of the decision for the employer. We were of the impression that a courts committee is in any case a rather odd kind of employer, being comprised of part-time magistrates who get together only on a rather irregular basis and who are only required to act in concert for ad hoc decision-making. The court clerk at Dalton (who had been a deputy at Woodgate when the application was made) took the view that he was starting afresh with a clean slate. He saw no need to affirm a commitment to equality by describing the court as an equal opportunity employer, believing such affirmations to be 'window dressing'. We formed the view that what happened in the court was very much the personal prerogative of the clerk. Consequently other courts may operate according to a quite different set of priorities and practices depending on the personality of the clerk.

Conclusions

We found little evidence of practical consequences as a result of this case. In so far as practices had changed at all, these were likely to have been regressive changes resulting in the exclusion of competent and qualified female applicants of child-bearing age from consideration. The case had, it seemed, only reinforced the clerk in all his prejudices about the risks of appointing females.

We believe that Dalton is unlikely to make the same mistake that its predecessor did and dismiss a trainee in the same circumstances, but this may only be because in recruiting new staff it avoids making appointments which it considers are likely to create problems.

Although the tribunal considered the fate of the applicant and advised the employer to reappoint the applicant, there was clearly scope for stronger practice recommendations to the employer.

D3: Trust Centre

The employer is a voluntary organisation with charitable status. It currently employs 2,500 people mainly in employment training programmes, and at the time of our research it was, in the main, reliant on government funding through the Manpower Services Commission. There is a headquarters staff of 120 with a senior management team of four. Two major unions are recognised for purposes of negotiating rights and about 80 per cent of HQ administrative staff are members of trade unions.

For this case study we interviewed the Director of the centre, the applicant and a trade union representative.

The decision

The tribunal found that the applicant had been unfairly dismissed by the employer in that, although the dismissal had been carried out for a valid reason, namely redundancy, the Centre had acted unreasonably by failing to consider the possibility of alternative employment for the applicant. The tribunal also found the employer to be in breach of the SDA in selecting the applicant for dismissal, when it found that a male employee was treated differently in similar circumstances. The applicant was awarded £1,700 as compensation for the dismissal and a further £350 in respect of injury to feelings arising out of sex discrimination.

The employer appealed the decision to the EAT but the decision of the tribunal was upheld. The EOC agreed to advise the applicant but not to give her further legal assistance or representation. She represented herself at the tribunal but employed a solicitor before the EAT. The employer was legally represented at both the original tribunal and the EAT.

Case history

The applicant had been employed by Trust Centre as an administrative officer for just over two years at the time of her dismissal. Since it was dependent on grant income to fund specific programmes of work, the Centre was required from time to time to make staff redundant when funding for specific programmes was not forthcoming or was cut back. About seven months after the applicant started employment the second administrative officer who worked alongside her at headquarters, and who had been appointed shortly after her, was made redundant, but was immediately offered and accepted alternative employment as a training officer. He was transferred without any break in his employment. The applicant took over many of the tasks previously carried out by the second administrative officer after his transfer.

About one year later another training officer post became vacant, and shortly after, the director discovered that further redundancies were going to be necessary. Discussions on how to manage these redundancies took place with the union representatives, and it was decided that four staff posts including that of the applicant would have to go. At that stage a union representative sought to intervene in the situation on behalf of the applicant by suggesting that the applicant should be transferred to the vacant training officer post as her former colleague had been at the last round of redundancies. However, the director took the view that the applicant was not suitable for this post.

The applicant felt aggrieved that she was being made redundant when there was a vacant post for which she regarded herself as suitable, but which she was not even considered for. She took the matter up formally with her union and further representations were made on her behalf to the director. The director continued to insist that the applicant was unsuitable for the post, but, unknown to the applicant, that the post had already been offered to another person without going through either an internal or external process of advertising. This new officer took up his post two weeks before the applicant became redundant. As a result of continued negotiations with management by the union on her behalf, the applicant was invited to apply for a new post for which the Centre had just received funding. The applicant agreed to apply for this post, but was not optimistic about her chances, since it was in an area of work where she had no experience. She applied, but as expected was unsuccessful. From the director's point of view this should now have been the end of the matter, as he believed he had tried to secure another post for the applicant. At this point, too, the union decided that it could do no more for her and the applicant left the employment of the Centre.

It is relevant to note here that there were very close links between union and management at the Centre, this being one of the complaints of the applicant. The director was himself a member of the same union as the applicant, and indeed he was a divisional office representative. It seemed that these links made it difficult for the union to take up the applicant's case. The applicant took the view that it was a union 'mafia' which ran the Centre, and that being male amounted to an entry qualification. The new training officer was, she believed, appointed through this grapevine. These perceptions of how the Centre was, in her view, mismanaged increased her resolve to pursue her grievance after she had left.

In arriving at its view that the applicant had been unfairly dismissed, the tribunal considered that the Centre should have looked internally to fill the vacant training officer post. It took the view that the applicant had the experience and qualifications which entitled her to consideration for that post, but that the recruitment was carried out in such a way as to preclude her from consideration. The dismissal involved sex discrimination because a male had earlier been shown preferential treatment when he was made redundant. In addition, the applicant had produced evidence of incidents involving sexist behaviour by the director in the past, and the tribunal was entitled to draw inferences from the fact that the employer's replies to the section 74 questionnaire were evasive and equivocal.

Effects and consequences

Although this was a dismissal case it raised as many questions about the employer's recruitment methods as it did about redundancy procedures. The director agreed that it would have been better to have advertised and interviewed for the disputed training officer post. He felt it was right that the Centre should be seen to be acting fairly. Nevertheless, he regarded interviewing as a 'rigmarole' because he generally knew whom he wanted for the post and it was, in his view, unfair to invite people for interview when this was the case. As a result of the case the Centre would be more inclined to advertise and interview. With the recent expansion in staff, there was now a personnel department which relieved him of some recruitment decision-making. As a result of the case things were now done 'by the book', and the informal approach formerly adopted by management, which he considered made for a friendlier and more relaxed working environment, had now been tightened up. The director had now learned that the proper way to have dealt with the affair was to have had an interview board for the training officer post, and rejected the applicant consequent to interview. This would have protected him from any accusation of unfair treatment.

However, the Centre took the view that despite the tribunal decision it had acted fairly and properly. It had lost the case because it had not been properly prepared, and no one, including the solicitor, had taken the time to get briefed up prior to appearance before the tribunal. In addition, the director felt that the chair of the panel, a woman, was biased against the Centre and had gone out of her way to be helpful to the applicant. Another panel might have found quite differently. For these reasons there was no need to over-react to the decision.

The case seemed to have had very few direct consequences for personnel practices. Apart from making greater use of formal recruitment procedures, the director did not believe that further changes were necessary. It was his view that there was no need to carry out any special review of the operation of the Centre's equal opportunities policies. The tribunal in his view had found unfair dismissal and thrown in sex discrimination for good measure, but the fact that the EOC had not 'supported' the case indicated to him that there was no real equality issue involved. In addition, the trade union had not supported the applicant and had exerted no pressure for change consequent to the decision. This latter point was confirmed by the trade union representative we spoke to, who believed that management would now put more effort into resolving disputes internally, and not allow things to reach the state they did with this case.

Conclusions
Despite having no success with the case at the EAT, the employer continued to believe that the decision had been a wrong one, and the failure of the EOC to assist the applicant and the lack of any follow-up action by the EOC only served to confirm the Centre's management in this view. The decision to tighten up on recruitment procedures and to play by the book was carried out almost vindictively ('I've tried to be nice to you but look where it's got me').

D4: Government department

The employer is a large department of central government with in excess of 10,000 employees. The department's personnel matters are the responsibility of its establishments division, which has policy sections dealing with issues such as equal opportunities and staff development and training in addition to administrative sections which deal with the affairs of particular staff grades.

For this case study we carried out interviews with two officers from the establishments division of the department, with an officer from the Office of the Minister for the Civil Service (OMCS) and with a trade union official.

The decision

The tribunal ruled that the department had discriminated against the applicant by imposing a requirement that she return to work on a full-time basis after the birth of her child. Such a requirement was judged to impose conditions which adversely affected women and with which the applicant could not comply, because of her duties to her child. The requirement disadvantaged the applicant in such a way that it could be construed as a detriment under section 6(2)(b) of the SDA. An appeal against the decision of the tribunal by the department was rejected by the EAT.

The applicant represented herself at a first hearing of the tribunal, a request for legal assistance having been rejected by the EOC. At a subsequent hearing and at appeal she was represented by counsel with financial support from her trade union. The respondent was legally represented at all appearances.

Case history

It took nearly two and a half years for this case to be resolved from the time of the originating application until the judgement of the EAT, one of the most prolonged cases in the sample. The applicant was employed as an executive officer by the department in a branch located outside Westminster. There were in excess of 1,000 employees in this branch, of whom 300 were executive officers employed on similar casework to the applicant. All officers at this grade worked full-time whereas, in the clerical grades below the applicant, part-time working was quite common. For example, about 25 per cent of clerical assistants had part-time contracts. This situation had come about due to an experiment conducted by the department to try to recruit suitable staff during a period of shortage. It was the view of senior officers in establishments division at that time that the experiment had not been a success and a decision was taken not to extend part-time opportunities to other grades.

The applicant had two children and was a single-parent. While she was on maternity leave for the birth of her second child she wrote to the department explaining that her position as the mother of two children would make it difficult of her to return to work on a full-time basis, and requesting that she be allowed to work part-time. The department did not discuss the applicant's request with her. Nor did it try to find out how many hours the applicant was seeking to work. Instead, a letter was written refusing the applicant's request and informing her that she only had the right to return under the same contractual terms as before. The applicant returned to work on a full-time basis, and shortly after submitted her application to the tribunal, but within two months of her return she went off on sick leave for a period of some six months.

There had been ongoing discussions within the department and throughout central government for at least 10 years prior to the tribunal application, about creating better opportunities for women within the civil service. In 1971 the Kemp-Jones report had noted that the expectation of an unbroken period of service from entry until retirement raised problems for women wanting to make a career in the service. The report recommended the expansion of opportunities for part-time working. More than ten years later a Joint Review Group of management and trade unions published a report on employment conditions for women which noted the failure of the management to implement the Kemp-Jones report and called for greater flexibility in contracts of employment and extension of part-time working to all levels in the civil service. This latter report had been published at the time of the first sitting of the tribunal and was referred to in evidence by the applicant.

At the tribunal the department had argued that less than full-time working was not possible for staff at the applicant's grade since the post involved casework and supervising other staff for which continuity of presence was essential. A manager in the applicant's office who was also a trade union representative gave evidence, however, that in his view part-time working by executive officers need not be a problem. In his view, and this was confirmed when we spoke to him, management had been dragging its heels over part-time working for years. It became clear during the tribunal that management had made no effort to find out whether the office where the applicant worked could have accepted her back on a part-time basis without disruption to office duties. In these circumstances, the tribunal took the view that without having made such an enquiry the department could not reasonably insist that the requirement to work full-time was justifiable. It became clear, too, that the applicant had all along been wanting to work four days per week rather than five. The department had made no effort to discover the hours the applicant wished to work and was therefore unable to estimate the amount of disruption her request would cause.

Effects and consequences

There has been a noticeable extension of part-time opportunities for women in the civil service since this decision. One problem is in discovering the extent to which the tribunal decision promoted these changes. It is necessary to record our view that if the request to work part-time had come from another officer, it is quite possible that it would have been treated with more sympathy than the applicant's request and might have been granted. The department was not opposed to part-time working as a matter of principle, but the position at the time seems to have been that it would only be granted at the department's convenience. This seems to have led to a situation whereby a request for part-time work would be entertained only if the officer's skills were in great demand or s/he was regarded by the department as a 'high-flyer'. The applicant was apparently not thought of as being in either of these categories and her skills and experience were seen as expendable.

There has undoubtedly been a change of attitude by the department to part-time working and while there is no automatic right for a woman to return to work after child-birth on a part-time basis, the philosophy now is that every request for part-time status is considered on its merits. We were told that since the tribunal the department has not turned down as single request for part-time working. The emphasis had now changed in the direction of trying to communicate with officers requesting part-time status to find out how the request could be accommodated. The department had produced a leaflet ('How to cope with changes in domestic responsibilities and still have a job') which was evidence of this change in emphasis.

There had been an active union campaign to keep part-time working on the negotiating agenda after the case. In addition, it was clear that the department was experiencing recruitment difficulties in various areas of work and more emphasis was being given to retaining existing staff on terms that were suitable to them. Greater publicity was being given to advertising the possibility of reinstatement for officers who resigned but wanted to return to work. The latest departmental figures showed that there were 900 part-timers up to and including grade 7 (principal) and 21 sets of job-sharers. We were unable to find out what jobs part-timers were doing, but the view was put by a union officer that these were unlikely to be in central policy-making areas.

There had been other developments aimed at making it easier for women to further a career. A job-share register had been set up following a staff notice asking officers to notify the department if they would like to be considered for job-sharing. Consideration was being given to setting up an 'in-touch' scheme for officers who had resigned or who were absent on maternity leave. Apparently, at least one other department operated such a scheme, and there had been a recommendation from the Management and Personnel Office (now the OMCS) that such schemes should be set up by departments. Aspects of an 'in-touch' scheme were, however, in existence and women on maternity leave were informed of their right to return from leave to attend promotion boards.

It is clear that in some areas there has been less progress. The civil service unions have been trying to negotiate with the department to have a formal agreement on part-time working which would protect the 'moral argument' for part-time work, if it became less of an economic necessity. So far the department has resisted such negotiations.

We should record that consequent to the case being resolved at the EAT the applicant now works as an executive officer on a part-time basis.

Conclusions

In an organisation as large and complex as a central government department, it is not entirely appropriate to look for the kind of response to a tribunal decision that one might expect with respect to a smaller, more cohesive work unit. Working patterns within the department vary considerably from one area of work to another and for different professions and career groups. A response which is appropriate for one set of career grades may not be appropriate for another.

It seems to be beyond dispute that the department has been considering a variety of ways in which the career prospects of women can be improved. A number of measures have been implemented, and attitudes have changed in such a way that the circumstances which gave rise to this case are unlikely to be repeated.

Pressure for change has come from different directions: through parliamentary scrutiny, through a tradition of active trade unionism, through women having a presence at senior levels, through encouragement and direction from the personnel office of the Civil Service Department and, not least, through the indignity of losing a case (or two) at an industrial tribunal and then having that indignity turned into embarrassment on appeal.

Other dismissal cases

In this section we analyse interview data with respect to five further dismissal incidents deriving from the secondary group of case studies. All the organisations considered here are in the private sector, although one of these is a non-profit-making trust.

D5: Chorley Motors Ltd

An industrial tribunal decided that the employer had discriminated against a male employee by dismissing him following his refusal to remove an ear stud. The tribunal took the view that the employer had applied to the applicant a requirement or condition which would not normally have been applied to a female employee. The applicant was awarded £550 by way of compensation of which £50 was a payment for injury to feelings. Both applicant and employer were legally represented at the tribunal hearing.

The applicant had been employed with the company as a van driver for a period of only four months before his dismissal, and so a claim under the EP(C)A for unfair dismissal was not possible. He decided to have an ear stud inserted, but this gave offence to his immediate manager who asked that it be removed on the grounds that it constituted a health and safety hazard, and because it was thought to reflect badly on the company image when he was visiting customers. The applicant refused to remove the stud and his refusal was brought to the attention of the branch manager who again asked him to remove it. After further refusal the applicant was dismissed. The applicant maintained that he would have been willing to remove the stud while at work but that it was necessary for it to be kept it in place for a period of three weeks to enable the pierced hole to heal. The employer was unwilling to countenance this line of argument.

The employer sought to argue under section 51 of the SDA that its action could not be construed as discriminatory because it had been done with the purpose of complying with another Act, in this case the Health and Safety at Work, etc., Act 1974, which imposed on employers a duty to ensure that there was an absence of risk to health in connection with the handling and transport of articles in and around the workplace. However, the tribunal took the view that an ear stud could not be said to constitute a hazard although pendulous earrings could be hazardous under certain working circumstances. It was clear that women van drivers wore earrings of various sizes in the course of their work, and this presented no problems for the employer. Had the applicant been a woman the employer would not have issued an instruction to remove the earstud, and he would not have been dismissed.

The company employs in excess of 5,000 people at various depots and garages throughout the country and has various semi-autonomous divisions which deal with car rentals, garage services, etc. It has a central legal department and it was here that the decision seems to have been made to contest the case on the basis that the company fights all such claims as a matter of policy. A case can thus take on a life and impetus of its own once removed from the immediate workplace setting. The company's legal department even instructed a barrister to present the case at the tribunal. The personnel manager expressed to us some regret that the company could probably have settled out of court for less money, but he had been advised by the legal department that the company had a good case under the health and safety legislation. As it was, the company regarded the award of £550 as 'not an inordinately large amount', and so there was no question of appeal. It was clear to him, however, that the applicant's immediate manager was the type of person who objected to men wearing earrings and that this was the real origin of the case.

The consequences of the case had been minimal. There had been a hint in the tribunal decision that the company's case would have been stronger, if there had been a company ruling about men not wearing earrings or studs, and consideration was giving to making a company rule to that effect in an attempt to prevent such a case happening again. However, the personnel manager came to the conclusion that the case was probably unique, and that making a general ruling was unnecessary. Although taken under the Sex Discrimination Act, this case will have had no impact on the employment situation or job prospects of the women who worked alongside the applicant.

D6: Carelle Kitchens Ltd

The employer makes, supplies and fits kitchen units from 30 outlets throughout the UK. It was until recently a small locally based company but has now been bought up by a large British multinational organisation which has new directors on the company board and has appointed a personnel officer. There is a workforce of some 300 directly employed by the company but many more who work for the company on a self-employed basis. At the tribunal the applicant represented herself and the employer was represented by a director.

The tribunal found that the company had discriminated against the applicant by dismissing her because she was pregnant. The applicant had been employed by the company as a part-time canvasser for some time, but, at the time of her dismissal, she was working full-time for the company as a receptionist at one of its branch offices. She had been in that post for only two months when she was dismissed. There was very little agreement between the applicant and the employer about the circumstances of the dismissal, and when we spoke to the personnel officer he continued to uphold the version of events presented by the company at the tribunal. This version was that the applicant had been dismissed from her employment because she was inefficient. The applicant's version was that when it became known shortly after she joined the branch as a receptionist that she might be pregnant, the branch administrator reported her pregnancy to a regional manager. Both of these officers apparently took the view that the applicant should have made it known to the company that she was pregnant at the time of her job interview.

The applicant believed that if there had been anything wrong with her performance, it should have been brought to her attention earlier, but no complaint had ever been made, and she had not received any warnings from the company about her behaviour. The applicant alleged that she had been told by a regional manager on a routine visit to the company that he was giving her notice because she was pregnant. When the applicant let it be known that she was considering the possibility of tribunal proceedings, she was later told by the manager that her dismissal was not to do with her pregnancy, but because of her general performance. The company insisted throughout its evidence that nothing had been said about her pregnancy. The tribunal seems to have had little doubt in preferring the evidence of the applicant, and found the employer's witnesses to be 'most unsatisfactory'. It took the view that the employer had dismissed the applicant simply because she was going to have a baby and for no other reason. The applicant was awarded £200 in remedy.

This was an example of a rapidly expanding company whose personnel policies and procedures had failed to keep pace with its economic growth. There had been some recognition of this problem in the decision to appoint a personnel manager who defined his task as being to come to grips with employment legislation. This appointment was not directly connected with the tribunal decision, but had more to do with the take-over of the company and the introduction of new management. There was a very low level of awareness of anti-discrimination legislation which had not been significantly heightened by the tribunal.

The company had put the case aside quite easily. As in other cases, we were told that the award had been so insignificant that the offence caused by the company's action could not have been grave, and the tribunal had offered no recommendations. If the breach of legislation had not been all that serious, there was certainly no need in the company's view to embark on a review of procedures. The company did not have an equal opportunities policy statement, and we were told that no thought had been given since the tribunal to introducing one. The personnel manager had not heard of the EOC.

D7: Wellmade Brick Co.

The employer is a small brickmaking business employing at the time of the dismissal only 12 people, six of whom were brickwork labourers, 3 men and 3 women. The applicant was one of these three women who were all made redundant together due to a downturn in the company's business and the lack of new orders. She was the company's longest serving employee having been with the company for 14 years and was the only one of the three women to submit an application to the industrial tribunal. She had lay representation at the tribunal, and the employer was represented by a solicitor.

Although both men and women worked on the brickmaking process as labourers, there was some differentiation of tasks, and the tasks performed by men and women had varied over the years depending on the type of kiln being used. The women had, however, at one time or another, carried out most of the tasks involved in the brickmaking process apart from two heavy tasks, namely, the transfer of raw materials into the mill and the crushing of raw material through the manual use of a hammer. When the employer realised that he was in a redundancy situation he took the view that it was necessary to retain only those members of the workforce who had the most flexible work skills. In his view, the male workers could do all the necessary tasks if required whereas the women were capable of carrying out only a limited range of duties. The decision therefore seemed clear, and all three women were made redundant.

After hearing evidence about the brickmaking process at other establishments, the tribunal formed the view that it was only by tradition that the women did not perform certain tasks. It was felt that they were capable of doing so, and evidence was given that the applicant would have been willing to have done a wider range of duties, if she had been asked to do so, and as she had done in the past when a different kiln was in operation. The tribunal's view was that the employer had failed to look at the relevant qualities, experience and length of service of each individual applicant and had looked on them as a class of employees to be treated in the same way. The dismissal had therefore been unfair. Consideration should have been given to the applicant's length of service, and to enquiring into her capability and willingness to perform the full range of duties. Had the applicant been a man she would have been treated on a more individual basis, and the method of selection for redundancy was therefore discriminatory. The applicant was awarded approximately £1,600 as compensation for loss of earnings and a further £500 for injury to feelings.

We interviewed the proprietor of the company who considered that the decision would have gone the other way if there had not been two women on the panel. The decision had not been a unanimous one and the employer's representative on the panel disagreed with the majority decision. However, being a small company on a very insecure financial footing he could not afford to appeal the decision. His instinct was to put the incident behind him and get on with trying to secure the future of the business. The only impact of the tribunal was to make him aware how difficult it was for a small business to comply with an enormous amount of employment legislation. He could not himself keep up to date with it, nor could he afford to employ someone to do so. It was cheaper in the long run to pay up if things went wrong. In his own mind he knew he had not discriminated against the women. It was simply that they had less all-round experience than the men and the most cost-effective solution was to make them redundant. When he found out that the applicant was taking a case to the tribunal, he had found it necessary to make a journey to the job centre to find out about the legislation.

D8: Samson and Co. Ltd

This is a small private company specialising in the treatment of dry rot, woodworm and other building infestations. The company has never employed more than 20 people and, at the time of the dismissal, there were only ten employees. The applicant was employed as an office administrator and had worked with the company for about four years. She claimed in her application to the tribunal that she had been unfairly dismissed and, in addition, been discriminated against in the way she had been dismissed. The tribunal found that she had not been unfairly dismissed but that there had been an element of sex discrimination, and she was awarded a payment of £100. Both applicant and respondent were represented by solicitors.

The company found that, due to an increase in the number of companies working in the timber infestation field, the amount of business was contracting and it had been required to lay off both surveyors and joiners. It became apparent to the director that a similar reduction might be necessary in office administration since in addition to the applicant he employed a junior typist who had joined the company two years after the applicant, and he felt overstaffed in the office in comparison with the amount of work to be done. It was the director's evidence that he had discussed his difficulties with the applicant and asked her if she would be prepared to work part-time in the future if it became necessary. He claimed that she had indicated that she would be willing to do so if it became necessary. The applicant denied having been involved in any such discussion of her prospects.

About this time the applicant became ill and there was a period of absence from the office of just over two months. The company found that it was able to manage its affairs without the applicant, and when she returned to work the director asked her if she would work part-time. She said that she would not be able to do so, having, she told us, recently taken out a mortgage. However, the director tried to persuade her of the benefits of working part-time by referring to the fact that she was a married woman with two children. In his view working part-time would give her the ability to devote more time to her children. The applicant continued to refuse to work part-time and was dismissed by the company by reason of redundancy.

The tribunal found that there had been no unfair dismissal because the employer had clearly been in a redundancy situation. The method of selection for redundancy had in its view been fair, and no agreed procedure had been broken. The employer could have managed without the applicant, but he had been generous in offering her part-time employment. In addition, the tribunal found that the fact that the applicant was a married woman with children played no part in the reasons for selection for redundancy. However, it was of the view that the director would not have sought to persuade a man of the value of part-time working by referring to his children, and that there had therefore been an element of discrimination in referring to the applicant's role as a mother. The tribunal considered that this discrimination was minimal and awarded the applicant £100.

The employer believed that the tribunal had really come down on the company's side by 'reluctantly' finding him guilty of sex discrimination. The amount awarded was less than the amount offered to the applicant in settlement prior to the tribunal. In his view, she had been a good employee, and he had found it difficult to make her redundant. He had only tried to make it easier for her by mentioning the benefits that might accrue if she went part-time. It had been a caring rather than a discriminatory remark and the tribunal, he believed, had perceived that this was how it was meant. The main effect of the case had been to make him more careful about recruiting employees. He had become 'hardened' by the case, since he had always believed he treated his employees well; he realised he would have to be more careful about who he took on, as he had not appreciated the applicant's capacity for what he saw as vindictiveness.

He had, he said, expected some follow-up from the 'women's equality people' but no contact had been made. He saw no need to make any changes although, if the tribunal had come out firmly against him, he would have taken it all more seriously. The applicant told us she had got another job in a solicitor's office soon after her redundancy. It was here that she had managed to get advice about how to pursue the case. She continued to feel very badly treated by the tribunal which, she believed, had failed to appreciate that she should have been retained in place of the other office worker who had been with the company for a shorter period.

D9: Clearways Trust Ltd

The employer is a registered charity which carries out building conservation work. Most of its income comes from donations or subscriptions, and it employs only two full-time permanent staff. The Trust has from time to time employed various people on Manpower Services Commission (MSC) sponsored training schemes, and the applicant was employed on one such scheme as a general building labourer. Being a member of the Trust, she had for some time done voluntary work, and had got to know the manager of the Trust who offered her work doing, among other things, bricklaying, when the MSC money became available.

However, within six weeks of her beginning work on the MSC scheme, the manager who had appointed her left the Trust, and a new manager was appointed to oversee the building works. His attitude towards the applicant was quite different, and he was less tolerant of her lack of bricklaying experience. Some of her work had to be done again and some youths working on the site who had even less experience of bricklaying than the applicant objected to having to take orders from a woman. The manager came to the conclusion that it was inappropriate for the applicant to be doing building work outside, since he thought the work was too heavy for a woman. He told her that she would have to leave and gave her the rest of the week off to find another job. The applicant took the view that if the manager had not been happy with her bricklaying, or with her ability to carry out heavy duties, he should have offered her other lighter tasks on the site, but no such offer was made. She believed it to have been part of her contract of employment made with the previous manager that she was only to be employed on light work.

In coming to its conclusion that the applicant had been dismissed because she was a woman, the tribunal also considered remarks made by the manager to the effect that he did not want any more women employed on the scheme. In the view of the tribunal the manager was opposed to women working on building sites, and this attitude had led him to seek the dismissal of the applicant. The tribunal formed the view that a man who had a contract which specified that he was to do only light work would not have been dismissed.

The tribunal made an award of compensation based on the amount of time that the applicant would have been employed had she stayed with the MSC scheme for the full year. She was awarded approximately £300 with another £50 for injury to feelings. No recommendation to the employer was made but the panel expressed the view that 'the respondents would no doubt be more careful in the way in which they approach similar situations in the future.'

We found no evidence that the attitude of the Trust had changed or that it had become more careful, despite the fact that another new manager was now in post. The scheme the applicant had worked on was no longer in operation, but the Trust was planning to participate in the Employment Training (ET) initiative and would in the future be carrying out work under that scheme. The new manager was a retired construction engineer, with views similar to those of the previous post holder, and he took the view that women should not be permitted to work on building sites. He said that if he had any control of the selection process for the ET schemes he would try to ensure that only men were taken on.

The findings of the tribunal had produced no positive effects. The decision had only served to reinforce the manager's views that employing women on building sites inevitably caused trouble. We concluded therefore that tribunal proceedings could perhaps do little by themselves to undermine such ingrained sexist attitudes. There is clearly a need for pressure to be exerted from other directions to ensure that training schemes operating with public funds comply with equal opportunity legislation and provide training for both men and women.

Summary: cases E5-E9

In this section we summarise the findings in relation to the five secondary group cases considered above.

Chorley Motors considered the incident to have been an isolated one, and therefore to have responded to the tribunal decision by issuing instructions or guidelines would have been, in the view of the company, an over-reaction. The applicant, a male, had been dismissed largely due to the attitude of the local manager, and not because of any company practice. The case had taken on a life of its own because the legal department had given what turned out to be wrong advice. It was unlikely that the company would ever react to a similar set of circumstances in the same way.

At Carelle Kitchens there had been rapid growth in the recent past but little attention had been paid to developing an effective personnel function, or to learning about the implications of employment legislation. This had begun to change but probably not as a consequence of the tribunal. The employer regarded the minimal award of £250 as an indication of the lack of importance the tribunal attached to the discrimination.

The director at Wellmade took some comfort from the fact that the decision had not been a unanimous one, and that the majority on the panel were two women whom he considered biased. He considered that he had not discriminated, and the employer on the panel was of the same opinion. The compensation awarded was the price a small business had to pay for falling foul of employment legislation. It had been an extra cost on top of the costs of making the women redundant, which he resented.

In a similar case at Samson the tribunal had found that the dismissal had been fairly carried out, and in the employer's view, this was an exoneration. The tribunal had been on his side, and this seemed to him to be clear from the meagre amount of compensation awarded (£100). The director believed there was no need to take any action apart from being more careful in future not to take on employees who might turn against him.

At Clearways the possibility of the tribunal's decision being studied for lessons to be learned was reduced by a change in management after the tribunal. The new manager was aware of the tribunal decision, but his attitudes towards women working in outside manual work were if anything more extreme than those of the previous manager. These views made it most unlikely that women would ever be employed again in the type of job the applicant had when she made the dismissal complaint.

Summary and conclusions

In this chapter we have examined the consequences of nine tribunal decisions, all but one of these being dismissal cases. Of the eight dismissal cases, four also included applications of unfair dismissal under the EP(C)A, and all but one of these four dismissals were found by the industrial tribunal to have been carried out unfairly under the terms of that legislation. The remaining four dismissal cases were brought under section 6(2)(b) of the SDA only, none of the applicants having been employed long enough to commence proceedings under the EP(C)A.

Section 6(2)(b) of the SDA states that it is unlawful to discriminate against a woman 'by dismissing her, or subjecting her to any other detriment'. In addition to the above eight dismissal cases, we have considered in this chapter a case of 'detriment', this being an application by a woman whose contract of employment required that she work full-time. All but two of the applications considered in this chapter were against private sector employers.

The application brought against the builders' and plumbers' supplier Dinkworth and Son was successful under both the EP(C)A and the SDA and the applicant, unemployed when we interviewed her, received approximately £1,700, although she felt that due to 'trickery' this was less than she was entitled to. The tribunal application had uncovered widespread dishonesty and corruption in the local branch where the applicant worked, and this resulted in a police investigation and a number of dismissals or resignations. A director took the view that this investigation would not have happened without the applicant's complaint. There had been some changes in personnel procedures following the case. Most notably, the procedures for dismissal had been tightened up, and employees were now informed of the company grievance procedure. The company had an equal opportunity policy statement, but the incident had not led to any review of the statement, nor of how it was put into practice.

The applicant who was dismissed by Woodgate Area Courts Committee when she became pregnant in a case brought only under the SDA received £1,200 by way of compensation. She was now happily employed in another career. It was unlikely that this employer (or rather the employer's successor) would dismiss anyone again in similar circumstances. However, the case had only served to reinforce reservations which the court clerk had about employing female staff, especially those of child-bearing age. It seemed likely that women who might become pregnant would be screened out through discriminatory questioning at a recruitment interview. The court did not describe itself as an equal opportunity employer, and no wider review of personnel policies had been carried out. Such a review was made difficult, however, because of a general reorganisation of the administration of magistrates courts in that area shortly after the application was made.

The case against Trust Centre was taken under both the EP(C)A and the SDA, and the applicant, successful on both counts, was awarded approximately £2,000. Since the tribunal had ruled that the applicant had been unfairly made redundant and that she should have been considered for another post which became available at about the same time, the attention of the tribunal was focused as much on the employer's recruitment procedures as on the dismissal arrangements. The employer was aware that the applicant would probably not have won the case if more formal recruitment procedures had been in existence. These had now been introduced, although with considerable cynicism on the part of the employer, and solely in an attempt to protect the Trust from future claims. The Trust had an equal opportunities policy statement but no review of this had been carried out. The employer set great store by the fact that neither the EOC nor the trade union had supported the applicant. This indicated to him that there was no real equality issue involved and that another decision could have been arrived at by a different (and, in his view, less biased) panel.

The application brought against the government department for refusal of a part-time contract of employment could have become a case of constructive dismissal, as the applicant was finding it increasingly difficult to carry out full-time duties, and was absent from work for long periods. Since the tribunal's decision there had been a considerable change of attitude towards part-time working in the department and indeed throughout the civil service generally. Within the department this had resulted in an extension of part-time opportunities, and no request for part-time working, we were told, had since been turned down. The unions saw scope for much more progress, and the extension of part-time work and other equal opportunity measures such as job-sharing were now on the negotiating agenda. The industrial tribunal decision and, moreover, the decision of the EAT would have played a part in this change of attitude, but pressure for change was being exerted from other sources as well. It could nevertheless be argued that the department's decision to contest the case even to the EAT was inconsistent with its claims to be promoting equality of opportunity.

In the remaining five secondary group cases two applicants (at Wellmade and Samson) were offered protection by, and made applications under, the EP(C)A in addition to the SDA. Both EP(C)A and SDA applications succeeded in the case of Wellmade, but the decision was not a unanimous one, and the employer felt he had been let off the hook. At Samson the unfair dismissal claim was not successful and the tribunal took the view that the sex discrimination had been minimal. Both of these companies were small family employers who considered themselves unlucky and the victims of embittered applicants and oppressive employment legislation. No changes were made by either employer. Clearways was also a small employer, although in this case a small charitable trust, making use of government-funded trainees for building works. It was unlikely to employ female trainees again if it could avoid doing so.

Carelle Kitchens and Chorley Motors were much larger employers. Carelle was in the process of trying to come to terms with a period of rapid expansion and was setting up a personnel function, but the company showed little inclination to learn anything from the case. There was a very low level of awareness of equality legislation. In the Chorley case, a male applicant had successfully used the SDA to establish unfair treatment by a local branch manager. There had been no change in company policy regarding dismissal decision-making so it was possible that such a dismissal could happen again. However, it was unlikely that a local manager would again be supported to the same extent by the company's personnel and legal departments.

In this chapter there have been a number of examples of employers who have sought to sidestep the wider implications of the tribunal decision by ensuring that they do not again employ women for the positions that have got them into difficulty. Sometimes an effect of losing the case is that the employer becomes even more entrenched in his attitudes and pursues a course of action (for example, excluding women from consideration for certain jobs) which is counter to good equal opportunities practice.

Such employers act in these ways knowing that it is unlikely that there will be any further scrutiny of their actions or follow-up after the tribunal decision. Some kind of minimal intervention at this stage by the EOC might reduce the likelihood of employers frustrating the tribunal decision. The tribunal itself could give greater consideration to the scope for recommendations since such recommendations might facilitate intervention by the EOC.

The absence of any intervention by the EOC during or after the case is certainly interpreted by some employers as an indication that the EOC have not been able to assist the applicant legally and few employers appreciate that such a failure to assist is not necessarily a comment on the merits of the applicant's case.

5 Equal Pay

Not all the cases in the research sample were brought under the Sex Discrimination Act, and in this chapter we turn to twelve cases brought before industrial tribunals under the Equal Pay Act 1970, as amended by the 1983 'equal value' regulations. In fact, only one case considered in this chapter is an equal value case, all others having been brought under the heads of like work or work rated as equivalent. One case considered here was brought under both the EqPA and the SDA and was successful on both counts. In another case the applicant failed to establish her entitlement to equal pay, but a related claim of victimisation on account of the equal pay claim was successful, and we have chosen to consider that case under the equal pay heading.

All but one of the cases considered in this chapter are against private sector employers. We follow the format of previous chapters by first considering in turn each employer in the group of primary case studies.

E1: Browns Ltd

This service sector employer has about 125 shop front branches on high streets up and down the country. Outlets vary in size from three to fifteen employees depending on the nature of the work undertaken. Some branches only receive work from customers and send it for processing elsewhere, while others both receive and process work on the premises. In total the company has about 750 employees on its payroll. There is a personnel officer at company headquarters and there are no trade unions.

For this case study data is drawn from interviews with a personnel officer, a sales director and the applicant.

The decision

The tribunal decided that the applicant was entitled to equal pay with her comparator having found that she was employed on like work. The employer had failed to make out a case that the variation in pay was due to a genuine material difference between the two jobs other than sex. The parties were allowed four weeks to arrive at an agreed amount of arrears, failing which a date would fixed for a new hearing to decide on the appropriate amount. In the event this proved to be unnecessary.

Both parties were legally represented, the applicant by a barrister and the respondent by a solicitor. The applicant's case was legally assisted by the EOC.

Case history

At the time of her application the applicant had been working for the company for some five years, initially as a sales counter assistant, but after acquiring the appropriate skills, as a multi-skilled branch assistant at the third largest of the company's branches. Her job was as a machine operator and processor, and being multi-skilled, she was expected to engage in at least three different types of skilled tasks. There was only one other multi-skilled operator in this branch, a male who had been with the company a few years longer than the applicant.

The applicant had been asked to do some work in the accounts department and while working on the accounts she discovered that her comparator was earning about £20 per week more than she was, her pay at the time of the tribunal being £76 and her comparator's £98 per week. The applicant brought this disparity to the attention of her branch manager but, in the applicant's words, 'she didn't want to know'. Following the company's grievance procedures, she then took the matter up with the district manager who refused to take any action. She wrote to the company sales director with no satisfaction and finally to the managing director. There followed a correspondence between the applicant and the managing director in which he sought to justify the disparity but the reasons did not satisfy her.

The applicant was not a member of a trade union (none were recognised by the company) but she enquired of a union which she knew was active in retail outlets. That union could not help her because she was not a member and finally, on the advice of her husband, she wrote to the EOC to seek advice.

There was a common pay structure throughout all the company's branches. This consisted of a basic weekly rate for the post held, and in addition, a merit allowance payment which could be up to 25 per cent of basic pay. Merit payments were, it seemed, at the discretion of the branch manager, but in awarding a merit payment the company took into consideration the personal attributes of the employee (such as his or her proficiency on the job, and willingness to work overtime and be flexible with hours) and the turnover and profitability of the branch. We heard from a manager that it was not unknown for branch managers to take into account the fact that a man might have a dependent wife and children when deciding how to allocate merit pay.

At the tribunal the company sought to show that, although the nature of the work done by the applicant and her comparator were similar in that they were both multi-skilled operators, the component tasks which each was required to undertake were quite different. It was claimed, for example, that the comparator was required to train new operators, to lift weights and to be more flexible about overtime hours. However, the tribunal found that overtime working was on a voluntary basis and could therefore not be considered as an integral part of the job; that, like her comparator, the applicant had in the past been engaged on training new operators and that she had lifted heavy weights when required.

In addition, the company sought to show that in the past the comparator's job had been as a supervisor. Although the post of supervisor had since been abolished it was claimed that his terms and conditions of employment had been 'red-circled' and that in the passage of time the anomaly between his pay and the applicant's would be levelled out. However, it was found that the disparity in pay predated the time when the comparator was appointed supervisor and the company produced no evidence to show that progress was being made towards levelling out the basic rates of pay of the two employees.

Effects and consequences

About one week before the hearing the applicant was offered a pay increase backdated for a period of about nine months. The proposed increase would still have left her worse off than her comparator and so she refused to cash a cheque sent to her by her employer for fear it would prejudice her case. On the day of the hearing the company's solicitor again made an offer to the applicant but this was declined.

Winning the case resulted in her getting a better deal than the employer was offering in settlement, and two weeks after the tribunal hearing she received the full amount of back pay, some £1,700. In addition, she was offered the title and pay of branch supervisor thus putting her on the same pay rate as her comparator. It will be recalled that the position of branch supervisor had been abolished some years previously, and it seemed that by reintroducing this post along with a new job description, the company was attempting to avoid related claims from multi-skilled female operators in other branches. The personnel manager told us of his concern that there would be other claims as a result of the applicant winning the case.

The applicant left the employment of the company to have a baby about ten months after the case and did not return. She made clear to us her dislike of the company, believing the wages to be very low and criticising the poor state of employer/employee relations.

There had been a number of important developments since the tribunal. First, the company took the view that the matter could have been resolved earlier without recourse to a tribunal if the district manager had informed his superiors of the applicant's claim. The district manager was judged to have acted improperly and was therefore demoted to branch manager. We were told that the company had been concerned for a long time about his performance and that this case provided an opportunity to take action against him. The applicant herself provided independent confirmation of his demotion.

Of greater importance, however, was the link set up between the company and ACAS officials which resulted in the company taking a look at ways of improving its bonus and merit pay system. It is likely that ACAS officials drew the attention of the company to the problems the merit pay system was causing, and we gained the impression that there would have been changes to the pay scheme even if the company had won this case. Nevertheless, immediately after the tribunal the company set up a committee whose remit was to work out a new pay scheme. Skills levels were defined, proper job grades were introduced and a new merit rating system was introduced within a year of the tribunal decision. Merit pay became a smaller proportion of an employee's pay packet and was decided at headquarters in accordance with a seven-point scale. The applicant confirmed that before she left the company everyone had been issued with a new job description and had been formally advised of a grade and merit rating. This had never happened in the past.

The scope for fresh equal pay claims seems to have been limited by these developments but we heard that two male employees continued to be paid at rates above the basic wage for their grade and that this was due to a previous 'red-circling' arrangement. We were informed that these discrepancies would eventually disappear due to the pay of the two men being held at current levels.

We heard that the company had had no other experience of sex or race discrimination cases. The company did not call itself an equal opportunity employer, nor had it sought to include any references to equality of opportunity in the staff handbook. The case had not precipitated any more general review of practice or procedure beyond the review of the pay structure. However, it was maintained that women did well within the organisation. Apart from the observation that both the sales director and the personnel manager whom we interviewed were women, we have no independent corroboration of that claim.

Conclusions

The intervention of the tribunal seems to have been successful not only in getting better pay for the applicant but also in setting up a new grading system and a method of merit payments which the company itself admitted was long overdue. Without the applicant having taken the case it is doubtful that any of these changes would have been introduced. ACAS played an important role in promoting these reforms, one of the few cases in this sample where we have been able to make such a comment. We note that ACAS was able to be of most help in giving advice to the employer about a new pay structure after the tribunal had come to a decision. We note, too, that it was the advisory service of ACAS, invited by the employer after the tribunal, rather than the conciliation service of ACAS which played a constructive role.

A company official was disciplined for mishandling the applicant's grievance but, as might be expected in an equal pay case, the tribunal decision had no noticeable impact on the development of equal opportunity policies within the company.

E2: Starpress Ltd

Starpress is one of a group of companies with common proprietorship in the publishing and communications industry. It is, however, operationally independent and has its own personnel function. At the time we carried out interviewing the company employed about 750, of whom 300 were skilled workers in the printing trades with only one of these being a woman. The remainder were unskilled workers and office staff. The company had recently come through a major rationalisation of its operations due to the introduction of new technology, and had lost about half its workforce. All employees are members of trade unions.

For this case study we interviewed the company's personnel director, a trade union representative and the two applicants.

The decision

The tribunal decided that the applicants, two female cleaners, were entitled to equal pay with male cleaners because their work was of a broadly similar nature. The company was instructed to pay the women the difference between their wages and that of a male cleaner backdated for a period of two years.

Both the employer and the applicants were legally represented at the tribunal and the applicants' case was legally assisted by the EOC.

Case history

The applicants were two of a group of about 10 female cleaners who were employed on a part-time basis by the company. They commenced work at 4 am and had generally left the premises by the time the working day began for other employees. The two women sought to compare themselves with male cleaners who were for the most part employed full-time by the company and who worked dayshift hours. The applicants had been unhappy with their rate of pay for some time and had from time to time let it be known that they thought they should be getting more money. The threat of redundancy had hung over their heads for some time and the rest of the workforce was being severely cut back. As cleaning staff left, they were not replaced and the applicants believed they were being asked to do an increasing amount of work for the same money.

The women had been aware for some time that their jobs were at risk, and there had been talk of contracting out the cleaning services.

By the time the applicants came to make a complaint to the industrial tribunal, they had in fact been made redundant and the company had contracted out the cleaning services.

The applicants had tried for some time to enlist the support of their union to pursue the complaint of unequal pay with management. Although a local union official had been sympathetic, senior officers of the union decided not to give the women support. This resulted in the applicants taking the union to an industrial tribunal in a separate development as they alleged that the failure of the union to support the equal pay claim against Starpress had prejudiced their chances of success and resulted in their receiving less compensation.

It should be noted that the practices of certain branches of the union had come under separate criticism from the EOC. The applicants had themselves been refused admission to the section which the male cleaners belonged to. Indeed they had experienced some difficulty in getting any section to take them on as members.

The applicants decided to raise their claim for equal pay directly with management through their supervisor. They allege that they were threatened with the sack and warned that their redundancy pay could be cut if they continued to pursue the equal pay claim. However, the applicants wrote to ACAS and were advised by ACAS to approach the EOC.

The company defended the case because it believed that the work done by the women and the men was qualitatively different. In reality, however, the company was concerned that, if it gave in to the claim, the elaborate structure of pay differentials which had been built up over the years would collapse and this would lead to a period of uncertainty in industrial relations. The union refused to back the applicants' claim for equal pay because it was believed the claim would lead to wider redundancies for cleaners throughout the industry. However, a local official of the applicants' union believed that the decision to contract out cleaning services had already been taken before the applicants took the case to tribunal. At the tribunal the company sought to prove that the job of a male cleaner which involved cleaning male toilets was more onerous than that of a female cleaner involved in cleaning female toilets. It was argued that the male cleaners spent more time cleaning toilets and that their jobs involved a higher 'obnoxious' element. In addition, it was claimed that the male toilets were used more frequently and that there were more of them.

However, the tribunal adopted the simple view that cleaning was cleaning and ruled in favour of the applicants.

Effects and consequences

The company was concerned that losing the case would make it vulnerable to claims from other quarters. Particular concern was raised about the scope for equal value claims since pay differentials in the industry could probably not be justified on any objective basis. The company therefore tried to avoid publicity about the case and engaged in what it described as a 'damage-limitation exercise'. Personnel directors from the various related companies got together to discuss the implications of the case and how they could prevent future problems. It was decided to speed up and broaden the contracting-out of all service jobs, and as a result, two other companies in the group decided to contract out cleaning services. We were told that Starpress would never directly employ part-time female cleaners again.

The company paid the women about £1,000 each in pay arrears. There was some difficulty in agreeing the amount and the personnel director took the view that the women had agreed to accept less money because they were getting 'cash in hand'. The applicants believed that they should have got more money but hoped to sort this out in their case against the union.

There were no more positive consequences to flow from the case either in terms of a general regrading exercise or in the direction of policy developments concerning equality of opportunity for women. There have been separate developments following an investigation by the EOC into membership practices in the applicants' trade union but we cannot comment on how effective this investigation has been in removing restrictive membership practices, or on how it will have affected, if at all, employment practices within the industry.

Conclusions

Apart from the fact that the applicants received back pay, and accepting that this may not have been the full amount due, there were no further constructive developments following on directly from this particular case. The organisation as a whole took defensive action to limit possible repercussions in related companies, and cleaning and other services were contracted out. The company claimed that as a result of the application it had been forced to take steps which in the long term would result in those women working in the industry losing out. For example, the company claimed that the rates of pay offered to women by outside contractors would be even lower than those which the company had been paying.

The company could have decided to retain the women and pay them the same rate as men. Instead it contributed to the lowering of female wage rates by seeking the same service at a cheaper price from an outside contractor.

E3: Northside Dealers Ltd

The company is a motor dealership, one of a group of eight dealerships throughout the UK trading under different names but under the same proprietorship. The group is in turn part of a wider network of companies with interests in the leisure and travel industry. Northside itself employs about 80 staff and has considerable operational autonomy, although personnel and industrial relations matters are the responsibility of a training manager based at group headquarters. It is one of the biggest dealerships in the group. Staff include motor vehicle mechanics and technicians, car sales staff, and parts department employees. Only about 25 per cent of staff, mostly motor mechanics, are in the trade union recognised by the company.

Data for this case study derives from interviews with the manager of the dealership, the parts manager, a trade union official and the company training manager.

The decision

The applicant made two complaints to the tribunal and both were heard at the same hearing. A complaint made by the applicant under the SDA that she had been dismissed by the employer due to her sex was rejected by the tribunal. However, it found her application for equal pay to be well founded in that the work she did was the same or broadly similar to that of a male comparator. The respondent was instructed to pay the applicant arrears for a period of nine months prior to her dismissal from the company.

At the tribunal the applicant was represented by a trade union official and the company by the training manager.

Case history

The applicant was employed by the company as a van sales driver. Her job involved delivering goods to customers and collecting cash on a route which had been allocated to her as one of four employees doing similar type of work. She had been provided with a written statement of terms and conditions of employment by the company and her letter of appointment stated that her job title was that of 'van sales driver'.

At the time of the annual wage review she was awarded an increase of 2 per cent, but she discovered that two male van sales drivers had been offered increases of 5 per cent. She discovered at the same time that the basic wage of the two men was higher than hers. She complained about this to the parts manager, but was told that, despite her job title, she was really a van driver and not a van sales driver. The manager told her that the men were expected to engage in selling parts for the company in the course of their rounds and they were therefore entitled to a higher wage rate. This claim was the essence of the company's defence at the tribunal.

A few weeks after the applicant complained to the parts manager she was dismissed from the company's employment after she refused to return to a customer to collect an unpaid account. The applicant complained that there had been sex discrimination in the way she had been selected for interview, but the tribunal did not find this to be so. She had been employed by the company for less than two years at the time of her dismissal and was therefore not entitled to proceed under the EP(C)A.

At the tribunal the company sought to maintain that the job title in the applicant's letter of employment had been wrong and that a mistake had been made by the company. However, when evidence was heard from the two male van sales drivers it became clear that selling was a very minor part, if any, of their job tasks and, in addition, the company was unable to produce any figure showing the level of sales obtained by the two men.

Effects and consequences

We heard from both the general manager and a trade union official who represented the applicant at the tribunal that she had received the full amount of back pay although we were not able to trace the applicant to verify payment details. One immediate repercussion of the case was that another female driver whose job title was 'van driver' rather than 'van sales driver' (although she maintained that she did the same as the applicant) had her case for equal pay with the male van drivers taken up by the union. This was granted by the company on condition that she agreed to take on exactly the same tasks as the men.

The training manager told us that as a result of the case the company had become more aware of the position of women within the organisation and they had therefore taken the opportunity to look at the rates of pay of male and female reception staff. He acknowledged that until the case male and female reception staff had been doing basically the same job but getting different rates of pay. The men had been called 'technical assistants' and the women 'clerical assistants'. Now they had the same job title throughout all eight dealerships and the rates of pay had been harmonised.

We were told that the circumstances which gave rise to this case were unique and were the result of an anomaly at this particular dealership. Work practices varied from one dealership to another and Northside had a greater amount of van delivery work than others. There were no obvious repercussions for other dealerships with regard to van delivery jobs. In the view of the general manager, the main outcome was that he had become much more aware of the need for clearly defined job descriptions. He maintained that the jobs of the applicant and the men had been different but the company's case had in his view failed because it did not have the documentary evidence to show that there were differences.

The training manager told us he had a remit for the promotion of equality of opportunity throughout the company. After the launch of the CRE Code of Practice senior line managers had attended a training course. From time to time he received booklets from the EOC which he passed on to local managers. The company had a policy statement dated four years prior to our visit entitled 'Race Relations and Equal Opportunities' which contained references to the SDA and EqPA. (It took several minutes of rummaging through filing cabinets before a copy was found!) A section from the policy statement is quoted in the staff conditions of service handbook which was found more readily. At Northside the general manager recalled having received a policy statement on equality of opportunity from headquarters but was unable to produce a copy after some searching. A staff conditions of service handbook was found. The general manager took the view that all staff must know about the policy because each was required to read and sign for his or her own personal copy of the handbook.

Conclusions

The tribunal resolved the disparity in pay between male and female van sales drivers. Although the applicant had been dismissed by the employer in connection, it seemed, with another incident, another woman doing a similar job had been granted equal pay with the male drivers. Furthermore, there had been a review of the position of female reception staff and differences in pay had been harmonised. The company had been made aware of the need for more detailed job descriptions, if only as a defensive tactic at any future industrial tribunals.

The company had an equal opportunity policy statement which had been unchanged for four years. The case had not led to a review of the operation of that policy.

The trade union had played an important role in pursuing the applicant's case and in following up on the implications of the case with respect to the job of another female employee. The union played this role despite the fact that neither of the two women was a member of the union at the time, although both agreed to join as a condition of obtaining union support. The constructive attitude of the union in this case contrasts sharply with the attitude of the relevant unions in the Power Supplies Co. and Starpress cases.

E4: Butcher Engineering Ltd

The employer is a light engineering company employing in excess of 1,000 workers nearly all of whom are based at one site. Butcher Engineering was described to us as a family run firm with close ties to the local community, it being one of the principal employers in the locality. The company recognises two unions both active in the engineering industry and these have full negotiating rights. About 70 per cent of the workforce are members of trade unions.

For this case study we carried out interviews with the personnel officer, a trade union official and the applicant.

The tribunal's decision

The applicant claimed that she was employed on like work with a male comparator who received a higher rate of pay. The tribunal found that the applicant was employed on like work with her comparator and that the company had failed to make out a genuine material difference defence. It ordered the company to pay the applicant arrears for a period of two years before the date of her application. An alternative claim that she was employed on work of equal value to two male comparators was not considered. The tribunal took the view that it would only consider the equal value claim if the 'like work' case could not be established.

The applicant was represented at the tribunal by an official of her trade union. The company was represented by an adviser from a branch of the Engineering Employers' Federation (EEF).

Case history

The applicant was employed as a tools control clerk and had been employed by the company for a period of about 11 years at the time the application was made. Her job was to supply tools from the company's stock of about 40,000 tools to sub-contractors engaged on work for the company. The job involved tracing the location of tools, checking on availability and logging them in and out. In addition, she had various residual duties and might be called upon to do typing in the office from time to time.

Her comparator had been with the company for some six years and also held the position of tool control clerk. At first his job had been identical to the applicant's except that he could not type and he was therefore allocated other clerical duties. As time progressed the tool control tasks became divided as a matter of convenience between the two clerks, with the applicant handling existing tools and her comparator handling new tools.

The applicant was a union representative and would on occasions attend meetings held at the premises. At one union meeting it emerged that the applicant was paid less than her comparator and the union decided that this discrepancy ought to be taken up with management. The applicant had the support of her comparator and he even gave evidence on her behalf at the tribunal hearing. The applicant told us that since the introduction of new managers industrial relations in the company had deteriorated. At one time there was very close cooperation with management and problems would always be sorted out by negotiation. The new managers had introduced batch production methods which the union thought were unsuited to the product and which had altered traditional working patterns. We got the impression that the case was pursued by the union as part of a wider campaign against new management practices. The applicant would not have pursued the case without the encouragement and support of her union.

We heard that the applicant and the union had exhausted all the recognised grievance procedures prior to raising an application to the tribunal. The company argued at the tribunal that it had become necessary to allocate a new task to the comparator which gave him a greater degree of responsibility and which justified the difference in pay. His job, it was argued, required a higher degree of technical skill because it involved the extraction of information from engineering drawings. However, the comparator gave evidence that it was a common-sense task requiring no special knowledge or skill. It emerged that the applicant was on occasions required to operate a VDU and the tribunal decided that such a task was of comparable technical complexity to consulting engineering drawings. The tribunal considered that the comparator's new task was in any event merely another aspect of the normal duties of a control clerk. The tasks done by the applicant and her comparator may have been different from time to time but they could all be subsumed under the general job description and terms and conditions of employment of a tool control clerk.

Effects and consequences

Within a few months of the tribunal decision the applicant had accepted voluntary redundancy from the company. The company decided to computerise the tool control procedures and the job of tool control clerk disappeared. She was offered alternative work but did not find it to her liking and declined the offer. She believes she was manoeuvred out of a job and that more interesting work could have been found for her if the company had wanted to keep her. In her view the company had wanted to demonstrate to others the consequences of taking the company to an industrial tribunal.

After the tribunal the company employed the EEF officer who had represented the company at the hearing as a consultant to advise on irregularities in the grading structure and where necessary to devise new job grades. However, it was clear that this exercise fell far short of a proper job evaluation scheme and that no major changes in the grading system had resulted. The purpose had rather been to discover if there were areas of work where the company might be vulnerable to further equal pay claims.

The personnel officer said the lesson had been learned that compromise was preferable to losing at a tribunal. He himself had been of the opinion that the company would lose the case; he had therefore advised senior management to settle but he had been overruled. He now believed his own position in the company had been enhanced and that alternatives to going the whole distance to a tribunal would now be looked at more carefully in any future cases. Another equal pay claim had in fact been resolved by negotiation.

The company did not have an equal opportunity policy statement and no consideration had been given to developing one. The company preferred to employ women in certain workshops where there was a tradition of female employment, industrial sewing being mentioned as an example. Much of the recruitment to the company still took place through informal methods. The company had in the view of the personnel manager a good local reputation and strong connections with the local community. Family connections certainly helped in getting employment with the company.

Conclusions

The case itself had no immediate impact for the jobs of other workers and there were no consequential equal pay claims. Both tool control clerk jobs were abolished shortly after the tribunal due to the introduction of new technology. The applicant was awarded back pay for a two-year period and with redundancy money we heard that this came to about £5,000.

The company had taken defensive action to deal with anomalies in the pay structure which it thought might give rise to further equal pay claims. However, there had been no detailed examination of the jobs done by men and women in the organisation with a view to creating a grading and pay structure which was free of sex bias.

Within the company there was a very low level of awareness of equal opportunity issues and there was no evidence that awareness had been raised by the tribunal's decision.

E5: Craft Casings Ltd

The company makes personal computer cases for a large well-known computer manufacturer. At the time of the tribunal the company employed about 600 people although due to expansion the number of employees was likely to increase to about 800 within the year. The company has five different sites all located in close proximity to each other and there was considerable transfer of personnel between sites. The company is part of a larger multinational group but is operationally independent both in terms of industrial relations and day-to-day commercial decision-making. There are no trade unions.

For this case study we interviewed the personnel manager and two applicants.

The decision

The tribunal found that all six applicants were entitled to equal pay with a male comparator. Each was awarded back pay amounting to approximately £400. The tribunal also considered an application made by some of the women that they had been victimised contrary to section 4 of the SDA by being denied opportunity for overtime working as a result of their equal pay claim. This application was refused. In a separate case the women also claimed that they had been unfairly dismissed by the company, and some women in addition claimed that their dismissal amounted to victimisation under section 4 of the SDA. A separate decision was issued on that application which later went to appeal, but we are concerned here primarily with the equal pay claim.

The company was represented at the tribunal by the personnel manager and the applicants by a solicitor. The case was legally assisted by the EOC.

Case history

The applicants were employed as power-press operators and spot-welders to work on a new order for the production of personal computer casings. The applicants' principal comparator had commenced work for the company some six months before the applicants. He had originally been employed on the paint-line, although as a result of changes in work patterns, and due to a reorganisation of work between the company's various sites, he was now mainly employed on the power presses. From time to time in the past some of the applicants had been required to work on the paint-line assembly.

The company maintained that the main comparator had specific training as a paint spray-gun operator which among other factors entitled him to a different hourly rate from the applicants. He was paid £3.23 per hour whereas the applicants were paid £2.35 per hour. The company maintained that this amounted to a material difference between his work and theirs, but the tribunal found that the comparator had not carried out this task since the last major reorganisation, and that the applicants and the comparator were now employed on the same or broadly similar work.

There were, in addition, other employees with whom the applicants sought to compare themselves. These were employed primarily as setters but the tribunal found that the work of these men was sufficiently different from that of the applicants, even although once the men had set the machines up, they then went on to operating tasks which were more or less similar to the tasks done by the applicants.

The company took the view that the women had been spurred on in their application by 'outsiders' (meaning, it seemed, the EOC). It maintained that it tried to sort out the women's claim in a constructive way by inviting the women to discuss the claim. In the company's view they were hostile and anti-company, and once they had involved the EOC there was no possibility of a settlement. The applicants remained very bitter about the company, claiming that there was no attempt to resolve their equal pay grievance. In their view, when the company was presented with the equal pay claim its immediate reaction was to try to engineer their dismissal. This it managed to do by transferring them to another area of work which the company knew was coming to an end. While there may have been a genuine need for redundancies, the applicants argued that the company took the opportunity to get rid of them, rather than other employees who had been taken on more recently, because they were regarded as troublemakers.

Effects and consequences
Even after the tribunal's decision the company still refused to acknowledge that there was any validity in the applicants' claim. The personnel manager believed that the tribunal had failed to understand

what it was like working in a factory where work patterns and routines changed frequently due to new orders being received. Employees could not expect to be engaged in the same tasks all the time, and they had to be ready to change jobs and sites when one consignment of work had been completed. In the view of the personnel manager, the discrepancy in wages had been due to men transferring to less skilled work (in this instance to the same work as the applicants) but carrying the wage rate for the old job with them. The company's expectation was that they would move back to their original tasks once these started up again. He said this 'red-circling' of wages could happen irrespective of whether the employee being transferred was a man or a woman (although in practice he could not think of any instances where women on a higher wage rate had been transferred to lower paid work but retained the old rate).

The main implication of the case had therefore been that the company had decided to introduce a limit on the period during which an employee's rate of pay would be red-circled. Consequent to the tribunal jobs would be red-lined after transfer to another area of work which normally attracted a lower rate for a maximum period of 3 months. After that period the person transferred would revert to the going rate for the job. This new system had apparently been put to the works council and had been accepted. The personnel manager told us he had taken legal advice which had given him the impression that a tribunal would be unlikely to entertain further claims for equal pay, if such a system was operational, and if a difference between a man and a woman's wage could be shown to be only a temporary arrangement.

At the time of our interview the dismissal and victimisation claims had not been finally resolved, but the women were of the view that they had lost their jobs due to the equal pay claim. Their dismissal would, they believed, serve as a warning to other employees and the company's action had, it was thought, warned other women off pursuing similar claims. Not surprisingly, the company claimed that the fact that there had been no claims from other women demonstrated that the applicants had been out on a limb and were troublemakers.

The company had no equal opportunity policy statement and had no plans to introduce one. Employees, we were told, got the same rate for the job irrespective of sex. About one third of employees were women who for the most part worked in the 'cable shop'. The personnel manager thought this was a good arrangement because women had 'nimble fingers' and making cables was not suitable work for men.

Conclusions

An important change had been introduced which would have reduced disparities in pay due to historic red-circling of wages. In so far as one consequence of red-circling was inequality of pay between men and women (as seems to have been the consequence in this instance), the effect of the new three-month regulation will be to reduce male wages rather to increase female wages. It is therefore not surprising that the company embraced the new regulation as a solution to pay parity problems since it also served to contain labour costs. This solution, however, offered no possibility of improving female wages in the company and it could therefore be argued that no wider material benefits have emerged from the case.

The applicants lost their jobs, they believed, as a result of the equal pay claim. This will have served as a warning to potential tribunal applicants about their likely fate should they pursue pay grievances in similar fashion. The company has a free hand since managerial power is not checked by trade unions.

E6: Hilling Council

The employer is an upper-tier local authority with in excess of 20,000 employees. The department of the council we are concerned with provides social care services to the area and has over 1,000 employees including professional and administrative staff. The department has its own personnel function.

For this case study, the only successful equal pay claim against a public sector body in the three-year study period, we conducted interviews with the principal personnel officer of the department, an officer of the council's central personnel section and a trade union official.

The decision

The tribunal decided that the applicant was entitled to equal pay with a male comparator and that the contract of the applicant should be altered so as to be not less favourable than the contract of her comparator. The employer did not seek to contest that the applicant and her comparator were employed on like work but argued that there was a genuine material difference between the applicant's contract and that of the comparator. The applicant was awarded a sum equivalent to the difference in remuneration between herself and her comparator for a period of two years prior to the date of the decision.

In a separate action following the decision of the tribunal, the applicant sued the authority in court for breach of contract in an attempt to recover loss of earnings for the years not covered by the tribunal's award. This action was successful.

The employer was represented at the tribunal by a solicitor and the applicant presented her own case.

Case history

The applicant was employed as a social worker by the council. She had previously been employed as a social worker by a town council, which we can call Marley, which following a reorganisation of local authorities was amalgamated into Hilling. It was part of the reorganisation package that Hilling would honour the terms and conditions of employment of the previous employer.

During the period of her employment with Marley the social work profession was itself reorganised so that those with a professional social work qualification became qualified social workers and those without became unqualified social workers. Different rates of pay applied to the two sides of the profession. The applicant did not have any of the recognised qualifications which automatically entitled her to become a qualified social worker, but there was an arrangement that those awarded a 'declaration of recognition of experience' would be admitted as qualified social workers. Following the reorganisation of the profession, the applicant received a letter of appointment which placed her on the qualified scale.

However, although the applicant had this letter of appointment she continued to be paid as an unqualified social worker contrary to the terms of the letter of appointment, and she continued to be described by the authority as unqualified. She complained about this and Marley entered into a special arrangement with her whereby she was paid at two points above the appropriate rate on the unqualified scale. The applicant was never fully happy with this arrangement: over the period of the following 10 years she continued to petition her employer, first Marley and then Hilling, to grant her qualified status but both refused. The employer claimed at the tribunal that, in entering into the special salary arrangement, the applicant had agreed not to pursue her qualified status claim. It was said that she had signed a document to this effect at the time, but the applicant denied having signed a document, and the authority was unable to produce it in evidence at the tribunal.

The position is, then, that the applicant had a letter of appointment from her previous employer appointing her on the qualified social worker scale. This contract was never put into practice, and she continued to be paid on an unqualified rate. She had been in dispute with her employer for years about this matter but the authority had refused to grant her qualified status. The case had even been considered by the director of the department who had personally refused her request. The dispute had soured the applicant's relations with the department for more than a decade.

The applicant sought to compare herself with a male who was unqualified but whom the department wrongly thought was qualified and who had been receiving the qualified social workers rate of pay until an application for promotion revealed his true status. It was the view of the authority's personnel officer that the applicant and the comparator had connived together to bring the case against the authority. The appearance of the comparator on the scene was fortuitous for the applicant, in his view, because it provided her with another avenue for pursuing her claim for qualified status and rates of pay. The authority's case rested on the fact that the comparator had been paid in error by the authority and that this amounted to a material difference in the contracts which justified the differences in pay.

The tribunal took the view that an error could not be held to be a material difference. In any case, there had been an error made with reference to the applicant's status which consisted in continuing to treat her as unqualified when she had a letter offering her a contract on the qualified scale. The authority had had many opportunities to rectify the error against the applicant but had chosen not to do so. It had gone along with a situation in which an error made in the case of a male employee had been allowed to operate to his advantage, but an error made in the case of a female employee had operated to her disadvantage. The authority had been unreasonable in allowing this situation to continue.

Effects and consequences

The applicant's contract of employment with the authority was unique. While the authority employed a small number (16) of unqualified social workers in addition to the applicant, none was in the applicant's situation of having received a contract of employment which had not been honoured, and none had entered into a special salary arrangement with the authority. The resolution of the case to the applicant's satisfaction and her pursuit of the case in the courts at a later stage had no direct consequences for the terms and conditions of employment of other employees.

The applicant's dispute with the authority and its predecessor predated the coming into effect of the Equal Pay Act in 1975 and it was only by chance when a suitable comparator appeared on the scene that the applicant was able to pursue a case under that legislation. It is perhaps worth noting, however, that all those who failed to gain qualified social worker status after the reorganisation of the profession were women.

As far as the authority was concerned the case did not raise any broader issues concerning equality of opportunity. There was an admission that the authority had been intransigent in the past and that a more enlightened authority might have resolved the case earlier. Instead attitudes became more inflexible as the years progressed, and the authority dug in its heels and refused to give in.

The decision did nothing to endear the tribunal system to the department's managers. In the opinion of the personnel manager, another tribunal would have come to a different view. The panel, of whom two were women, chose to support the applicant because it had, in his view, feminist sympathies, and was looking for a case to uphold. The panel's sympathies prevented it from appreciating the merits of the department's case. The whole process may have hardened managerial attitudes on equality issues but we had no evidence that attitudes on these matters had been particularly progressive or forward looking prior to the tribunal.

The case seems to have had no impact at all on the progress that the authority had been making towards implementing an equal opportunity policy. The tribunal was seen as a purely internal departmental matter with no wider implications for the authority. Since the case the authority had come under the control of the Labour Party which had a manifesto commitment to promote equality of

opportunity. Some elements of that policy such as the esta
of a women's committee had already come into effe
programme of training was about to be set up for all those in . ╌╌╌ ╌╌ ╌╌╌
recruitment and training.

Conclusions
The applicant's long-standing grievance against the authority was
successfully resolved by her use of the equal pay legislation. Her
success at tribunal allowed her to pursue a case against the authority
in the ordinary courts and to win that case as well, although she had
to pay her own court costs to do so. It is arguable whether she would
have succeeded in court without the tribunal decision behind her. The
decision must have given her the confidence to pursue matters further.

Other equal pay cases
We now turn to the remaining six equal pay cases in the secondary
group of case studies. As in previous chapters we consider each
employer in turn and summarise our conclusions about the group at
the end of the section. The employers are all private sector
organisations, five being commercial organisations and one being a
voluntary body.

E7: Chestertons Ltd
This is the only equal value case in the sample. The employer is a
furniture maker and a case was brought by 23 female machinists who
claimed that their work as machinists was of equal value to work
carried out by male upholsterers. The workforce had been contracting,
having fallen from a peak of almost 400 employees in the 1970s to
only 120 at the time the claim was made. Most of the shop floor
employees were members of a small trade union active in the furniture
business. The applicants were represented by counsel and were
legally assisted by the EOC. The employer was represented by an
industrial relations advisor.

Female machinists and male upholsterers were on the same basic
rate of pay, but, some years prior to the application, the male
upholsterers had managed to negotiate an allowance of 16 per cent on
top of the basic rate on the grounds that they were now doing heavier
work and working in more congested surroundings. The tribunal
asked an independent expert to decide whether the work of the two

groups was of equal value. The expert's report concluded that the work of the women was at least of equal value. The skills required were about the same and, although the men's tasks required greater physical effort, the women's tasks were more complex. The report concluded that the men's tasks were worth 15.5 points and the women's tasks 16 points.

The company did not challenge the expert's report and conceded that the jobs of the applicants and the male upholsterers were of equal value, but it sought to show that the difference in contract was due to a material factor other than sex. The company sought to show that because the weight of finished products had increased and because the upholstery workshop had become congested due to an increase in the volume of work, it had become necessary for the company to pay upholsterers the extra 16 per cent as an incentive to retain them in employment.

However, the tribunal found that no work study was carried out at the time the allowance was awarded to enquire into whether the female machinists might be similarly entitled to such an allowance. At the time the allowance was awarded there was no objective evidence available of any material factor amounting to a difference in the work carried out by the male upholsterers which justified the disparity. It arose because the men had negotiated the allowance and the women had not and for no other reason.

As a consequence of the case the system of allowances was harmonised and machinists were put on the same system of allowances as the upholsterers. In addition, the company had to find two years back pay for the 23 applicants at a cost of £20,000. The applicants agreed to accept payment in two stages to ease the company's cash flow problem.

After the applicants' success the remaining machinists who had not joined in with the original claim made applications to the tribunal for equal pay. The company won some of these cases but lost others. We were told by the chief executive of the company that, due to skilful stalling of the case by the company, by the time the second round of cases were heard, the women had been on the harmonised rate of pay for some time so that the amount of back pay was proportionately less because of the two-year rule.

There had been no equal value claims from other groups of workers, although the possibility of further claims seemed to exist as only the machinists and the upholsterers were paid the new harmonised rate.

E8: Higgins International

The company is the UK subsidiary of a multinational electronics company whose headquarters are overseas. The British workforce consists of 130 employees involved only in sales and marketing, as the company has no production sites in the UK. There is no trade union organisation at the company's present site. Internationally the company employs about 30,000 workers.

The applicant had been employed as a personnel officer with the company for a period of three years up to the time of her retirement. She took retirement when the company transferred its UK offices to a site which it became inconvenient for the applicant to work from, and a new personnel officer was employed in her place. Prior to working as personnel officer the applicant worked as secretary to the managing director, and when the previous personnel manager retired the applicant took over as personnel officer. In claiming equal pay the applicant sought to compare herself both with her predecessor, the personnel manager, and with her successor, the new personnel officer who took over on her retirement. The applicant was represented by counsel and was legally assisted by the EOC. The employer was represented by an official of the Engineering Employers Federation.

A pre-hearing assessment had ruled that the applicant could not in law compare herself with a successor, but at the full hearing the panel set aside that view and decided to hear both claims. It found that the applicant did not do like work with her predecessor as there were substantial differences in qualifications and in the level of decision-making. The applicant had been appointed as personnel officer to carry out a job which was different from the job undertaken by her predecessor.

The tribunal took the view that Article 119 of the Treaty of Rome entitled the applicant to compare herself with her successor, a male who had been appointed on a salary higher by some £2,000. The company did not seek to contest that the applicant and her successor did like work. Its case had been that comparison with a successor was not possible under the EqPA and that a company ought to be allowed to pay a successor a higher rate of pay if it was necessary to attract the best person for the job. The tribunal therefore ruled that the applicant was entitled to equal pay with the successor.

This case seems to have been pursued with a view to establishing a legal precedent. This fact was appreciated by the employer who claimed that he would be aware in the future of the risk of employing a man on a higher salary to replace a female, but he saw no need to take any other action consequent to the decision. There had been no attempt to review the company's salary structure nor had the tribunal given any hint or indication that this was necessary.

E9: New World Schools

The employer is a religious organisation which runs private schools throughout the UK and elsewhere. The applicant was a teacher in one of these schools and had been employed by the organisation for about six years. She applied to an industrial tribunal, having been refused a home owner's allowance by the employer who considered that as a married woman she could not be regarded as a head of household. She compared herself with a male teacher and colleague who had successfully claimed the allowance after the appropriate qualifying period. The applicant was legally represented at the tribunal and her case was assisted by the EOC. The employer was represented by a regional director. Membership of trade unions is not permitted by the organisation.

The applicant was a married woman whose salary was the main source of household income. Her husband was self-employed and contributed to the household only an irregular income. The employer had a scheme for its teachers whereby those who were purchasing a house on a mortgage and who had five or more years experience were entitled to qualify for a home owner's allowance of £180 per month. The applicant wrote to her employer claiming the allowance when she became entitled to do so by length of service, but her claim was refused in a letter which told her that 'inasmuch as you are a married woman and being supported you are not eligible'. The letter went on to say that the allowance was only payable to heads of household.

The tribunal found that the employer's rationale for paying allowances was based on assumptions which were discriminatory against women. The system of allowances assumed that only men were heads of household. In the view of the tribunal it was wrong to assume that men were more likely to be the primary income earners for the household. The tribunal found that there was no material difference in the work done by the applicant and her comparator and that the applicant was therefore entitled to receive the allowance. She was awarded arrears of payment amounting to over £3,000.

We heard from the employer's regional director that there had been previous complaints about the way the allowance scheme was operated and that the matter was due to be discussed at a national level at the time the applicant raised the complaint. The applicant had been assured that even if the matter was not resolved to her satisfaction by the national council he would undertake to change the allowance system within the region. He had asked the applicant to wait for the outcome of the national conference but she had not felt able to do so.

The regional director was not surprised by the tribunal's decision. He claims to have used the decision to good effect to persuade the national organisation to change the terms of the allowance scheme. Since the decision, allowances have been awarded to male and female employees irrespective of sex or marital status and without any enquiry into whether there were other earners in the household. Employees only had to meet the qualifying period of five years service. Between 40 and 50 employees were immediately affected by the change in policy and all these were now paid the allowance.

E10: Motorbox Ltd

The company makes gear boxes for motor vehicles. It employs about 350 people on two sites and there is a print room at each site. Two female applicants working in the print room on one site sought to compare themselves to a male worker at the other print room who earned almost £1,000 a year more. The applicants were represented at the tribunal by a union official and the respondent by an industrial relations director.

Two years prior to the application to the tribunal the employer had carried out a job evaluation exercise and job descriptions were produced for each employee, although it seems that these were never issued. The job evaluation exercise had rated the jobs of the applicants and the comparator as being of the same value, each being awarded 197 points. When the applicants became aware that their jobs had been rated the same as that of the comparator but that they were being paid less, they approached their trade union representative who drew this fact to the attention of management. An interim payment was made to the applicants pending the final outcome of the job evaluation process and its implementation.

Following the report of the consultants who had carried out the evaluation and awarded points to each job, it was envisaged that as a next stage the jobs would be placed in salary grades and specific pay rates would be allocated to each job. However, this second stage was never carried out, and it was the view of the tribunal that salaries were subsequently fixed in an arbitrary manner without regard to the points system produced by the consultants. We heard that there had been a change of management after the first stage of the evaluation exercise and it was the view of the company at the tribunal that it no longer made commercial sense to carry through the consultants' report to the next stage.

The employer sought to argue at the tribunal that the comparator's job had become materially different from that of the applicants since the evaluation, but the tribunal did not accept that the employer had presented convincing evidence that some of the tasks had become more onerous and more frequent compared with those on the basis of which his job description had been produced. The panel therefore concluded that the employer had failed to prove that the difference between the salary of the applicants and that of their comparator was due to a material factor other than sex.

One of the applicants told us that the union had pursued the case on their behalf because the company had failed to honour the agreement made at the time of the interim award. The company had been taken over by new managers who had refused to carry out the second stage of the job evaluation scheme. The tribunal had forced the company to implement the scheme and she was therefore happy with the outcome. As far as she knew there had been no other claims following the decision. A manager confirmed that the anomaly between the two print rooms had been rectified. However, work patterns had changed to such a degree that the job evaluation scheme could no longer be fully implemented. The company would look carefully at any further claims for harmonisation but no further evaluation of jobs was planned.

Case E11: Wellmans Ltd
Wellmans is a small company of less than 15 employees which imports and distributes health foods, vitamin supplements and cosmetic items

from abroad. The company's headquarters are overseas where all of the manufacturing is carried out. By tradition the manager is sent by headquarters to Britain, but all the other employees are local people. The applicant submitted an application under both the EP(q)A and section 6(2)(a) of the SDA claiming that she had been denied access to the opportunity for promotion. She succeeded on both counts and was awarded approximately £2,250. Both parties were represented by solicitors and the applicant was legally assisted by the EOC.

The applicant worked as a packer in the warehouse where her job consisted of filling bottles with vitamin pills and packing, handling and storing boxes. She worked alongside a man who was first employed by the company at about the same time as the applicant but who earned more money than she did. The applicant sought to compare herself with this man, claiming that she did like work.

After working alongside each other for a period of some 18 months the comparator left Wellmans and took employment elsewhere. However, within two months of leaving he returned to Wellmans having been invited back by the manager to take over the post of warehouse manager which had recently been vacated by another employee. The applicant believed that she was entitled to be considered for promotion to the job of warehouse manager, since she was working for the company when the post became vacant, and because she had been acting as deputy to the warehouse manager before he left. She also claimed equal pay with the now returned comparator for the period dating from when he started back again with the company.

The applicant thus sought to compare herself with the same man but during two separate periods of employment. The company resisted comparison for the first period on the grounds that although she worked alongside the comparator, the comparator was required to do heavy lifting which the applicant, nearing retirement age, was not capable of doing. However, the tribunal accepted the applicant's evidence that she frequently lifted heavy weights and awarded her equal pay for the first period of comparison. It decided that during the second period after his return to the factory as warehouse manager, the comparator carried out work which was substantially different from the applicant and that there were therefore no grounds for equal pay for the second period.

The tribunal also found that the applicant had not been informed that the job of warehouse manager was vacant, and that the company had denied her the opportunity of applying for the job. It took the view that she had not been told about the job or invited to apply because the manager considered the job to be a man's job involving the lifting of heavy weights. The tribunal came to the conclusion that the reason the applicant had not been invited to apply for the job was because she was a woman. The panel considered that she would have had a one-third chance of securing the job had she applied, and she was awarded one third of the differential in salary payments for the relevant period. The applicant continued to work for the company for another two years until her retirement.

Since the tribunal a new manager had been put in post by the company. The applicant suggested that the former manager had been removed because he mishandled the situation, but the new manager said he had been removed because of the poor trading position of the company and because he had been a bad communicator. The new manager claimed her style was quite different and that all problems were now discussed in a more open manner. She took the view that the applicant had been unsuitable for the job of warehouse manager due to her age, but that the previous manager could have handled the situation with more sensitivity.

Apart from the fact that the applicant had been put on a higher rate of pay, there were no wider changes. The new manager said she would have to be more cautious about employment legislation, but she took the view that in a small company there was no room for fixed work patterns or rigid job descriptions: everyone had to be prepared to be flexible and this was explained to new recruits when they arrived. In such a situation there was always the potential for disputes among employees.

The applicant told us she had received her award but only after a long period of time. The company paid her the amount in two stages claiming that there were cash flow problems. She had expected to receive more money from the tribunal, and she had in fact turned down a larger amount offered in settlement by the company through ACAS.

Case E12: Grants Builders Ltd
The employer is a large construction company which builds houses for private sale. It employs about 400 people including an

administrative staff of about 90 and a sales team of 25. The company is part of a larger group of companies which we can call Grant Holdings, and which consists of about 15 companies employing in total over 1,000 people. The applicant was a sales negotiator with the company, and she brought a claim for equal pay with a male whom she regarded as employed on like work. She also brought a claim under section 4(1)(d) of the SDA claiming that she had been victimised by her employer as a result of making a demand for equal pay, in that her hours of employment had been reduced from five days of work to two.

The applicant's claim for equal pay was rejected by the tribunal, but the employer was found to have victimised the applicant. The applicant was awarded £100 by way of compensation for injury to feelings and a further £725 in lost earnings as a result of a reduction in hours. In addition, the tribunal recommended that the applicant be restored to a five-day working week. The applicant was represented by a solicitor, and her case was legally assisted by the EOC. The respondent was represented by an industrial relations consultant.

The applicant worked on site as a sales negotiator showing potential purchasers around properties and arranging the preliminaries of sales contracts. In common with most other members of the sales team, the applicant had no contract of employment even though she worked a 30-hour week and was considered to be a full-time employee. The exception to this state of affairs was the position of three male employees who had contracts and who worked on a salary and commission basis. The applicant's view was that she was doing the same job as one of these salesmen, but getting paid much less, and she became involved in discussions with other female staff about how to improve their terms and conditions of employment. The applicant and other employees took advice from the EOC and sought a meeting with one of the company's directors. They related their grievances to him, including a claim for pay parity with the male sales staff and a request for proper contracts of employment and job descriptions.

The director took the applicant's grievances to the chairman of the company and, it seems, lobbied on the applicant's behalf for equal terms and conditions with the male sales staff. The chairman turned down these representations, and it was shortly after this meeting that the applicant was told her working days were to be reduced from five to two.

The tribunal rejected the applicant's claim for equal pay on the grounds that, had the company operated a grading system, the comparator would have been on a much higher grade than the applicant due both to his previous track record in sales and to the expectations which the company had of him. However, the tribunal decided that the applicant's working hours had been reduced due to the fact that she had been the spokesperson for the women's grievances, and had come to be regarded as a troublemaker by the company.

The chairman of the company confirmed to us that the applicant had received compensation, and that she had been returned to a five-day week as recommended by the tribunal. However, the company required her to work weekends which she found inconvenient and which probably amounted to further victimisation, and she resigned within a month of going back to five-day working. It was clear to us that the chairman was quite glad she had gone voluntarily. Indeed, he took the view that it would have been more appropriate to have dismissed her when she made the initial protests. It had been a mistake to keep her on at all.

There had been no changes in the terms or conditions under which other employees worked. The majority of the sales staff were still part-timers without any contracts of employment or job descriptions, and the company was not prepared to alter the status of these workers, as it took the view that giving them contracts would make the company vulnerable under employment legislation. Contracts of employment were regarded as privileges to be extended only to the most valuable employees (all of whom were male). The company had refused to consider the wider question of pay inequality on the sales team. In the chairman's view pay equity was the 'small print' of employment legislation which he had no time for. Equal pay laws interfered with his right to manage, and we were told 'there's no question of equal pay for anyone'.

It seemed that following the case the status quo had been maintained with the added bonus for the company that the applicant, who in the view of the company had caused all the trouble, had now departed.

Summary of cases E7-E12

Chesterton's had harmonised the allowance system for upholsterers and machinists and £20,000 had been paid out in back pay. There were subsequent claims from machinists not included in the tribunal application, and this had resulted in further payments by the company. However, there were no further claims from other occupational groups, although it seemed that there might have been grounds.

The success of the claim against New World Schools resulted in about 50 other employees being paid allowances subsequent to the applicant being awarded arrears of £3,000. The tribunal decision seems to have been used constructively by a sympathetic manager to encourage the organisation to change the allowance system throughout the country.

At Motorbox the tribunal decision was instrumental in bringing into effect those aspects of the job evaluation exercise which affected the applicants and the comparator. This had been financially advantageous to the applicants. There had, however, been no implementation of the findings of the exercise as a whole.

The retiring personnel officer at Higgins won her claim for equal pay with a successor, but the case seems to have been presented in order to establish a legal precedent and not primarily with a view to encouraging the company to examine pay and conditions. No such examination was conducted by the company.

A new manager had been installed at Wellmans and this might have had something to do with poor personnel management by the previous occupant. The applicant continued to work for the company for a further two years prior to retirement and reported no victimisation. There were no consequences for other employees who each negotiated separate terms and wages directly with the manager.

There had been no improvement in the terms and conditions of sales negotiators at Grants, and the applicant left the company shortly after the tribunal. The chairman of the company was opposed to all employment legislation and particularly to any notion of pay equality or job contracts. The prospects for any improvements in these matters looked very bleak.

Summary and conclusions

In this chapter we have considered a group of twelve equal pay cases and tried to discover what the implications of these cases have been for pay and conditions and for job grades within the organisations concerned. Where relevant, we have also sought to comment on the implications of the decision with respect to the development of equal opportunity policies. Eleven of the equal pay applications were brought against private sector organisations, with one of these being a voluntary non-profit-making body. Only one application was against a public sector organisation and this was a local authority. In eight of the twelve cases applicants were legally assisted by the EOC.

At Browns we discovered that the tribunal decision was instrumental in bringing about important changes in the grading system, and in getting a new pay scheme off the ground. It was likely that these changes would have been introduced even if the employer had won this case, since ACAS had performed a valuable advisory role in pointing out deficiencies in the pay structure even before the hearing took place. New job descriptions were issued following the review of the grading system. In addition to receiving back pay, the applicant gained a new job title in recognition of the tasks she had in fact been performing. She had, however, since left her job to have a baby and had not returned. A district manager had been demoted for his mishandling of the applicant's grievance.

The two applicants at Starpress were awarded pay arrears, but there was some dispute as to whether the amount paid by the company was the full amount. The applicants had in any case been made redundant by the company prior to their application being lodged, but after it became known that they were seeking pay parity. Not only were the applicants made redundant but so also was the rest of the company's cleaning staff. Cleaning services were contracted out in a move designed to head off claims from other workers which might disrupt pay differentials in the industry. Similar action was taken by other companies belonging to the same group. This case of itself did not have major implications, but, coupled with a subsequent case the applicants raised against their trade union and an investigation conducted by the EOC, efforts to promote equality of opportunity within the industry seemed to have been stepped up.

The applicant at Northside Dealers was no longer working for the company. She had been dismissed shortly after her application for equal pay, but in a manner which the tribunal found did not amount to sex discrimination. She had received pay arrears, and another woman employed by the company in a similar job had received equal pay as a result of the tribunal decision when her case was taken up by the union. As a result of this case the company had examined the pay of reception staff, and introduced pay equality for men and women in these grades. The company had an equal opportunity policy which had been drawn up several years earlier, but there had been no review of the policy as a result of the tribunal's decision.

Butcher Engineering had employed a consultant after the industrial tribunal to carry out an analysis of its grading system, but this had been done with a view to ensuring that there were no areas where other equal pay claims might be imminent. No specific job evaluation exercise had been conducted with a view to ensuring pay parity between men and women. The applicant had received back pay, but shortly after the tribunal her job was abolished, and she accepted redundancy after having been offered unsuitable alternative employment. She took the view that she had been squeezed out as a result of her pay claim.

The applicants at Craft Casings believed that they had been dismissed due to their equal pay claim, and this has resulted in a separate application to the tribunal. Despite a vindictive and hostile attitude, the employer seems to have taken steps to eradicate some of the conditions which gave rise to the claim, by introducing changes in the arrangements for the 'red-circling' of jobs. A higher wage after transfer will now be maintained for a maximum period of only three months. It was likely that the real motive for such a change was the financial saving that would be made by the employer, rather that any sudden conversion to introducing equitable pay arrangements.

The case taken against Hilling Council was peculiar in that the applicant's grievance against the authority predated the arrival of equal pay legislation. The EqPA provided a vehicle for her to pursue with success her claim for qualified social worker status. The tribunal decision opened up the way for a successful action against the authority in the courts. There were no obvious implications for any other employee of the authority.

We have already noted that the decisions against Chestertons and New World Schools had implications for other employees beyond those making the initial claims. Both cases involved systems of allowance payments which operated in a discriminatory manner. At Motorbox the decision had a more limited impact: the applicants had succeeded in getting the employer to implement the findings of a job evaluation exercise for their own jobs, but there had been no wider implementation with respect to other employees. We concluded that at Higgins International the case had been used to establish a legal precedent, and that there were no implications for other company employees. Wellmans was a small business where a change in management may have led to an improvement in management-employee relations, thus lessening the likelihood of a similar incident reoccurring. The management at Grants remained inflexible after the tribunal and no attempt was made to address major shortcomings in the terms of employment of the female sales staff.

Employers frequently sought to characterise an industrial tribunal as a unique event which had no further implications or consequences. In some instances, they took this view because of the failure of the panel to sketch out the implications of the decision for employment practices. In other instances, they accurately perceived the implications but were reluctant to face up to them. In a few instances there was no obvious general lesson to be learned nor practice worthy of closer inspection.

It is always possible for employers to be looking at ways of developing equal opportunity policies, but a tribunal case may not necessarily raise the issues which are most relevant or pertinent for a particular employer. The fact that there has been an equal pay case against an employer does not necessarily mean that lack of pay parity is a major problem which the employer ought to be addressing.

There is greater scope in equal pay cases than in sex discrimination cases for affecting the circumstances of a substantial number of employees. Even though a sex discrimination case may reflect directly on the equal opportunity policies of the employers, the case itself generally relates to the grievance of only one particular applicant. Some equal pay cases come about through an isolated female employee comparing herself with a group of men and in such cases the implications may be limited only to that employee. But more frequently a victory for the applicant has immediate repercussions for other employees.

Perhaps for this reason and also because they concern 'bread and better' matters to do with pay and conditions, trade unions are likely to find themselves involved more directly in equal pay cases than in sex discrimination cases. As has been shown, however, they do not always intervene to support the applicant if there are conflicting concerns about the maintenance of pay differentials.

Tribunals have no authority to issue recommendations to employers in equal pay cases, that power being restricted only to breaches of the SDA. However, it seems reasonable to expect employers to have regard to any implications the case might have for the extension of equality of opportunity, particularly if it is a case which the employer knows that the EOC has been assisting. For example, losing an equal pay case could lead an employer to look at inconsistencies in job descriptions or in the way jobs are evaluated and graded. Any such examination might enhance the value of women's jobs within the organisation and consequently improve their scope for reaching more senior grades.

The scope for evasive behaviour by the employer is probably as great in equal pay cases as it is in sex discrimination cases, especially if there is no trade union organisation, or if the trade union has been unsupportive of the applicant. Such evasive behaviour is most likely where more than one employee stands to benefit from the tribunal decision, and where losing the case may have serious financial implications for the employer. Whole areas of female employment have been contracted-out and jobs which are vulnerable to equal pay claims have been reorganised or mechanised to undermine the possibility of further claims. By and large, however, it is easier in an equal pay case than in a sex discrimination case to demonstrate the objective gains that have been obtained by the applicant in pursuing his or her grievance to a tribunal.

6   Conclusions

This study has looked in detail at the responses of 40 employers who were found by an industrial tribunal to have breached sex discrimination or equal pay legislation. We have sought to discover whether losing a case at a tribunal has been an incentive for these employers to take remedial action to deal with the source of the discrimination, or to examine current employment practices, or to act to promote equality of opportunity within the organisation.

The responses of these 40 employers have been considered in four chapters each of which addresses a different type of discrimination, namely in recruitment, in promotion, in dismissal and in pay. The methods of research have been for the most part qualitative, that is, we have conducted in-depth interviews with key participants in the process, and have used this research data to illustrate what happened within the organisation as a result of the tribunal decision. A summary of the impact of tribunal decisions is presented at the conclusion of each chapter where the effects and consequences for each employer have been considered in turn.

Our research questions have been formulated in the light of previous research carried out by Alice Leonard, in particular her investigation of the effects of successful industrial tribunal cases on applicants[1]. Our own study has focused on the effects of cases on employers. Taken together, the two studies provide a picture of the overall effects of industrial tribunal decisions.

This concluding chapter has three sections: in the first we quantify by way of further summary the changes in policy, practice, attitude or behaviour which occurred amongst the group of 40 employers; in the second, we examine the influences which assisted or inhibited change;

and in the third, we make our assessments of some of the implications of the findings.

Summary of changes

Attitudinal changes

The degree to which an employer adopted more progressive attitudes as a consequence of the tribunal's decision has been assessed. Clearly we have not been able to measure changes in attitude in any systematic or rigorous way, but we have tried to arrive at an indication of whether or not the process of being taken to a tribunal has made the employer more supportive of an equal opportunity programme. Such attitudinal shifts do not, of course, indicate that any practical measures will necessarily have been undertaken, but it could be argued that the adoption of a positive outlook is a precondition for any practical equal opportunity initiatives taking root in the organisation.

Table 5 summarises some of the aspects of change considered in this chapter. Attitudinal changes are considered in column (a). Attitudes became more progressive after, and because of, the tribunal decision in the case of 7 employers (17 per cent). They deteriorated and the organisation became more hostile towards the promotion of equality of opportunity in 5 cases (12 per cent). Attitudes were unaffected for the remaining 28 employers (70 per cent).

All except one of the employers where we detected more progressive attitudes developing were in the public sector, the exception being a voluntary organisation, Homebuild (P10), and four were promotion cases. By contrast, all but one of the five organisations where attitudes had worsened as a result of the case were private sector employers. Unlike the 'progressive' group the majority of those where attitudes had deteriorated were equal pay cases, and there were no promotion cases.

We should offer some reservations in relation to the group of employers where attitudes had become worse. First, at Jones Outlets (R2) attitudes had hardened at a local branch level only and not, it seemed, at headquarters. The same could be said of Hilling Council (E6) where central management was pursuing a progressive equal opportunities policy. Even at Craft Casings (E5) where management took a hostile view, some changes had been introduced.

We can conclude then that only in a minority of cases did the tribunal actually make attitudes worse. For a significant minority, nearly all in the public sector and therefore subject to equal opportunities pressures from other sources, attitudes became more progressive. But for the majority the tribunal had no effect on attitudes one way or the other.

Equal opportunity policy initiatives

Some employers had adopted an equal opportunity policy statement since the industrial tribunal application. Column (b) of Table 5 shows that the tribunal decision was at least partially instrumental in bringing about the adoption of a formal equal opportunity policy in eight cases (20 per cent). No employers told us that a policy had been set up as a direct result of the tribunal application (an employer may have been reluctant to say so even if such had been the result) although the closest to a cause and effect relationship were the cases of City Council (P1), a non-party political council, and Homebuild (P10).

In most of these eight cases the tribunal decision was contemporaneous with other developments. At Denton Council (R1), for example, the development of a policy was being discussed some time before the tribunal, an initiative which coincided with a change in the political balance of the council. At Jones Outlets (R2) an equal opportunities policy statement was introduced seven months after the tribunal, but a manager said that the Codes of Practice had been more influential than the tribunal. At Carlton Council (P2) a new political initiative had led the council to become an equal opportunity employer, but it was likely that several adverse tribunal decisions had had a cumulative impact. Similar considerations were important at both Frinkley Council (P6) and Easterly RHA (P7), both organisations having been affected by other tribunal decisions and subject to political pressure. At Ford Council (P8) a change in the political complexion of the council was clearly an additional factor which facilitated change.

Six of the eight organisations which had introduced equal opportunity policies were public sector employers, and six involved promotion or transfer applications.

These findings suggest that an adverse tribunal decision is rarely a sufficient incentive on its own to become an equal opportunity employer but that it can play a part among other influences in moving employers in that direction.

It might be expected that, consequent to the decision of the tribunal, those employers who already had a policy statement would be persuaded to review the statement with the aim of reformulation or elaboration. Seven employers claimed to have an EO policy statement prior to the tribunal and one other (P5 Shepley) referred to itself as an EO employer in advertisements (but had no written policy statement).

However, there was little evidence that industrial tribunal decisions led to review of existing equal opportunity policies, (see column (c)). Foodcheck (R7) saw no need to review or amend its policy after the tribunal, since it regarded the decision as having no wider significance. Promoting equality of opportunity was now a lower organisational priority for Shepley (P5), and no re-assessment of its self-ascribed 'equal opportunity employer' status was carried out. Power Supplies (P3) had had a sketchy policy statement for some years prior to the tribunal, but the wide-ranging review carried out by the company could better be explained by the EOC's intervention through the joint exercise. A government department (D4) claimed that its EO policy was always under review and it employed staff to carry out this function, but it was not possible to say that the tribunal had itself led to any reformulation of that policy. Dinkworth (D1), Trust Centre (D3) and Northside Dealers (E3) had paper policies, but in none of these organisations were these re-examined as a result of the tribunal.

Disciplinary action against the discriminator

Employers can demonstrate a commitment to change by taking action against those who have discriminated. Disciplinary action by the employer against the discriminator may be appropriate if the employer has a policy statement which informs employees of their liability and of the likelihood of disciplinary action in the event of breaches of the legislation. Very few employers in our sample were in such a position. Furthermore, the discriminator may be an official in an organisation with a culture of tolerance towards discrimination (as, for example, in Paper Supply Co. (R8), Starpress Ltd (E2), Grants Builders (E12)), or s/he may be a senior official or the proprietor (for example, Northern Tools (R4), Popham Plastics (P9), Clearways Trust (D9)). In other instances, the organisation may not have the authority to deal with the discriminator, most obviously perhaps when non-employees are brought in to participate in the appointments process, as happened with councillors and school governors at Frinkley Council (P6) and magistrates at Woodgate Area Courts Committee (D2).

Nevertheless, as shown in column (d), disciplinary action connected with the circumstances of the application was taken against employees in six organisations (15per cent). Shepley (P5) reprimanded two chief inspectors who may, in addition, have been encouraged to take early retirement. A manager at Power Supplies (P3) who wrote a note containing sexist remarks had, it seemed, been demoted even though the company argued that the remarks had not influenced the selection process. At Ford Council (P8) those involved in the interview were reprimanded. In the other three cases the links between the discriminatory activity and the disciplinary action were more tenuous: at Dinkworth (D1) employees were sacked but as a result of wider misdemeanours uncovered in the course of the dismissal application; at Browns (E1) an equal pay claim provided an opportunity to demote an unsuitable manager, while at Wellmans (E11) the case may have contributed to the manager having been moved on.

Recommendations to employers under section 65 of the SDA

Formal recommendations to employers can be made by tribunals only in cases brought under the SDA and not in equal pay cases. Thus recommendations could have been made in 30 cases (including two cases brought under both the SDA and the EqPA). In fact formal recommendations were issued as part of the tribunal's decision in only six cases, 20 per cent of those eligible. To what extent do employers carry out recommendations?

At Denton Council (R1) a recommendation to include a woman on the subcommittee was carried out, but another to set up a working party was judged impractical and was not pursued. The tribunal recommended that City Council (P1) offer the applicant a promoted post within two months of the tribunal and this was carried out in full by the council. Shepley Transport Co. (P5) was advised to interview the applicant at the next promotion board and if she was not successful at that board to give her written reasons for her failure to be appointed. There was conflicting evidence as to whether there had been another promotion board since the tribunal, but the applicant had not been interviewed and remained unpromoted at the time of our interview.

A recommendation was issued to Power Supplies (P3) to review its interviewing procedures, to include a woman on interview panels (but 'where practicable' provided a convenient escape clause), and to vary the composition of interview panels more frequently. The company remained hostile to these recommendations and took advice on their legal status. Interview procedures had been reviewed, but the company had no intention of including a woman on interview panels, and there was no requirement in the revised interview procedures introduced for bringing more variation to the composition of panels.

A government department (P11) was advised to take action (which the tribunal did not specify) to ensure that the applicant could take up the appointment. The department had acted to change transfer procedures with a view to decreasing the likelihood of others coming up against similar obstructions, but, it seemed, the applicant remained in her previous post. Grants Builders (E12) were recommended to restore the applicant to five-day working. They did this but also insisted that she work weekends and she left their employment.

It is a practical precondition for making effective recommendations that panels appreciate and understand the origins of discriminatory actions and before making a recommendation have fully analysed the likely effects on the organisation. Many panels are not capable of issuing recommendations because they have a poor grasp of the issues and do not have this appreciation and understanding. Here it is the grasp of the issues that has to be addressed and improved and not merely the failure to make recommendations. Some employers react constructively to advice and suggestions which fall short of recommendations. It is the tribunal's ability to make links between the specific breaches of the legislation and more general failings of policy, practice or procedure which provides the basis on which useful recommendations or suggestions can be made.

From our reading of tribunal decisions it appears that some tribunals are reluctant to issue recommendations unless these are asked for by the applicant or her representative. The tribunal is more likely to respond with a recommendation if a case for it is put forward.

Specific actions consequent to the tribunal

Column (e) of Table 5 lists the organisations that made specific practice changes and Table 6 lists in summary form the specific measures taken by employers as a result of the decision of the tribunal.

We have excluded from this list the various effects considered above, that is, changes in attitude, changes brought about as a result of recommendations made under section 65 of the SDA, disciplinary actions against employees and developments in equal opportunity policy statements. Nor are actions taken by employers to give effect to remedy, such as compensation awards, included. The effects considered under this heading are therefore voluntary changes in practice or procedure which can be directly related to the matters considered by the tribunal. It is unlikely that these measures would have been carried out if the applicant had not taken the employer to the industrial tribunal.

Seventeen employers (42 per cent), eight in the public sector and nine in the private sector, had taken specific measures to deal with the issues raised by the application to the tribunal. Examples of such measures included changing the procedures for issuing application forms to job enquirers, sending copies of the tribunal decision to key people in the organisation, issuing a circular on the main points of the decision, using the decision in a training programme, issuing a leaflet to employees, introducing a new pay scheme.

Some measures were more effective than others and not all of them went to the root of the problem. For example, the impact of a circular or memo issued after a decision would be dependent on its tone and the terms in which it was couched (whether it was an instruction or advisory only), and on other factors such as the seniority and status of its author. We have therefore made an assessment of likely impact and effectiveness and tried to distinguish between measures which had, or were likely to have, only a cosmetic or limited impact and those which were more fundamental in scope. In six of the seventeen cases we judged the measure to be cosmetic or of limited impact only and these are identified by italic print in Table 6.

Factors influencing change

Representation

Previous research has shown that applicants who are represented at tribunal are more likely to win cases than applicants who present their own case[2]. There may also be a link between representation and the likelihood of follow-up action by the employer. Unfortunately we do not have enough cases to arrive at a firm conclusion on this point. However, we identified eight cases where the tribunal resulted in or contributed to the employer developing an equal opportunity policy. In all these cases the applicant was legally represented by a solicitor or by counsel. Furthermore the applicant was represented in all the six cases which resulted in recommendations being made by the tribunal (in one of these six cases she was represented by a trade unionist). S/he was represented in all six cases where disciplinary action was taken against specific employees. S/he was represented at some stage of the proceedings in all seventeen cases where specific practice or procedure changes were introduced by the employer. (In the government department (D4) she was represented only at the appeal stage.)

It should be emphasised, however, that there were only six cases where the applicant was not represented at any stage of the proceedings (see Table 4, page 13) and so no conclusive evidence on the importance of representation can be presented. Nevertheless there does appear to be a pattern: in none of the cases where the applicant represented herself did the employer introduce an equal opportunity policy, discipline any employees or make specific practice or procedure changes. In not one of these cases were recommendations issued by the tribunal.

EOC assistance

In 20 cases (52 per cent) the applicant received legal assistance from the EOC. Was such assistance an encouragement to employers to engage in follow-up action? First, we can note that the applicant was legally assisted by the EOC in the cases against four of the seven employers who had adopted equal opportunity policies after the tribunal and in ten (59 per cent) of the 17 cases where employers made specific practice or procedure changes. In addition in four of the six cases where employees were disciplined the applicant's case was assisted by the EOC. There is therefore some ground for believing that legal assistance improves the possibility of a constructive response by the employer.

It can be argued that representation, and especially representation which is provided through the assistance of the EOC, is effective because the applicant is enabled through skilled advocacy to counter the explanations of the employer and improve his or her chances of winning the case. In addition, the applicant is enabled through reasoned argumentation and analysis to elucidate and expose the practices in which the particular act was grounded. In this way the employer's failings become more readily apparent both to the employer himself (whose understanding of the issues may in consequence be better developed), and to the tribunal panel which is more likely to be able to make constructive suggestions and to give pointers for follow-up action.

Size of employer

It is a striking finding that large employers were more likely to have taken action following an industrial tribunal decision than small employers, since it means that more people were likely to have been affected by the changes adopted. Organisations with more than 1,000 employees made up 45 per cent of the sample (see Table 1, page 11), but accounted for 70 per cent of those which had made practice or procedure changes after the tribunal, and six of the seven (86 per cent) which had adopted equal opportunity policies. In addition, the largest employers were more likely than others to appear among the small group of employers (seven only) who were identified as having adopted a more progressive attitude towards equality of opportunity.

There was no evidence of a particular tendency among large organisations to take disciplinary action against employees, but few if any conclusions should be drawn from this as there were only six cases in the sample where disciplinary action was taken. Larger organisations are more likely to have complex decision-making procedures and communication patterns which make it more difficult to pinpoint the origins of the discrimination.

Public/private sector differences

Public sector bodies had a higher representation than expected among organisations where there had been follow-up action consequent to the tribunal. The public sector accounted for 30 per cent of the sample; but four of the seven organisations to have adopted an equal opportunity policy and just under half of the seventeen organisations which made consequential changes in practice or procedure were in the public sector. It was clear, however, that private sector organisations had not been inactive after the tribunal. In addition, such organisations were more likely than those in the public sector to have taken disciplinary measures. However, all but one of the organisations which were identified as having adopted more progressive attitudes were in the public sector.

Type of case

The tribunal decision was more likely to have had an effect in promotion cases than in any other type of case. For example, of the eight organisations setting up equal opportunity policies, six had lost promotion cases; of the seven organisations where there had been a beneficial change in attitudes, four had lost promotion cases; and of the four organisations to take action against the discriminator, three had lost such cases. In addition, there was a good chance that an organisation losing a promotion case had made specific practice changes.

Effects were least likely in equal pay cases, but this was to be expected since the issue considered by the tribunal was a narrower one and organisational practices did not always come under scrutiny to the same extent as in a sex discrimination case. On the other hand, it should be noted that equal pay cases were often conjoined with, or closely related in time to, a sex discrimination application (E3, E5, E11, E12), and this suggests that the applicant's grievances in such a case were not solely connected with pay.

Effects may be most likely in promotion cases because of the continuing pressure of the applicant within the organisation, especially if she or he actively seeks to campaign for changes (P1, P6 and to a lesser extent P2 and P7). But seven of the eleven organisations which lost promotion cases were public sector bodies which, as already noted, had a better record than those in the private sector for taking follow-up action.

Appeal cases

Only five cases (P7 Easterly RHA, P10 Homebuild, D2 Woodgate, D3 Trust Centre, D4 Government Department) resulted in an appeal to the EAT and no obvious pattern of effects and consequences emerges from an inspection of this group. Appeals may be more likely in cases which are not legally assisted by the EOC as the applicant's case is likely to have been less well argued. On the other hand, a well presented and argued case may raise contentious intepretations of the law which become grounds for appeal. In cases D2, D3 and D4 the applicant had no legal assistance from the EOC.

Implications

Our case studies have shown that employers may be encouraged to change their practices in relation to the employment of women following the adverse findings of an industrial tribunal in a sex discrimination or equal pay case. We need to bear in mind, however, that our study was confined to a group of cases where the applicant was successful. Such cases are a minority of all formal complaints of sex discrimination and equal pay. Further research would be needed to determine how far unsuccessful complaints and cases that were conciliated differed in their impact upon employment practices.

Moreover, in order to understand the impact of tribunal decisions, it is necessary to be aware of the broader context within which organisations engage in any reassessment of policy and practice. For such reassessments to happen there need to be both incentives and resources to carry them out. For many employers, and especially for the smaller ones, practices change from day to day in response to issues and problems as they arise. Policies do not exist in any explicit and codified form.

The following point has been made in an assessment of the impact of unfair dismissal tribunal cases on employers:

> The incentive to change policies, procedures and practice will depend in large part on the perceived advantages to be gained by so doing and the likely consequences of not doing so ... Where advantages are not perceived the likely consequences of inaction are not such as to provide a strong incentive to change[3].

Such an observation is just as relevant to other discrimination cases as to unfair dismissal cases and many of the positive steps taken by employers which have been observed in previous chapters can be attributed to a recognition by employers of the likely advantages, such as expected improvements in the industrial relations climate within the organisation, or expected improvements in the motivation of women employees once sources of job discrimination are removed. Similarly, inaction is likely if the employer assesses that the chances of further complaints to an industrial tribunal are negligible or are worth bearing.

It would be a mistake to assume that applications to industrial tribunals are made only against employers with poor records on equality of opportunity. Employers who have taken some steps towards equal opportunity policies may also be the target of applications because there is likely to be a greater awareness among their employees of the scope for pursuing discrimination cases, and such employers may create a more favourable climate which facilitates the filing of a claim. In addition, an employee may feel the more offended by unfair treatment to the extent that the employer claims to have an equal opportunity policy.

Section 65 of the SDA defines the powers of the industrial tribunal to intervene in the employment practices of an employer and limits recommendations to measures which are directed at 'obviating or reducing the adverse effect on the complainant of any act of discrimination to which the complaint relates'. This formulation would seem to indicate that practice recommendations must be directed at improving the prospects or employment situation of the applicant, and must have a bearing on the nature of the complaint being considered by the tribunal. The tribunal is therefore seriously restricted in its capacity to propose far-reaching practice or procedure changes even when serious omissions or defects have become apparent in the course of the tribunal's examination of the facts of the case.

If any practice recommendation proposed by the tribunal has to be restricted to reducing 'the adverse effect on the complainant', the tribunal, it seems, has very little scope for making recommendations in either recruitment or dismissal cases when the applicant has never been, or is no longer, an employee of the respondent. (It could perhaps be argued that the recommendations made to Denton Council (R1), a recruitment case, would have affected the applicant if she chose to apply for another job with the council at a later date.) Even in cases where the applicant is still an employee of the organisation, for example in promotion cases, it is not clear whether the action proposed has to be specifically aimed at the applicant (as in the case of Shepley Transport (P5) where there was a recommendation to interview the applicant at the earliest opportunity), or whether a broader interpretation of section 65 directed at having an impact on a group of employees of which the applicant is only one (as in Power Supplies (P3)) is the correct one. It will be recalled that Power Supplies took advice about the legal status of recommendations and as a result decided to ignore them.

Such limitations on the powers of the tribunal would seem substantially to restrict its scope to influence the behaviour of employers especially when it has become clear that a practice has discriminatory consequences and that the applicant was a representative of a class of people any of whom were likely to have fallen foul of a particular discriminatory requirement. For example, it seems that a tribunal which has found an employer to be in breach of the SDA by operating an age bar on recruitment which had the effect of discriminating against a married woman would have no powers to order that such an age bar be removed generally within the organisation. When a tribunal has engaged in a thorough examination of the facts of the case in such a way that serious inadequacies in the employer's recruitment, selection, dismissal or promotion practices have become apparent, the tribunal should be at liberty to make recommendations without having any obligation to demonstrate that the recommendation will be of direct benefit to the applicant.

Given the infrequency of discrimination cases in the volume of work which industrial tribunals undertake, the ability of tribunal panels to build up an expertise in anti-discrimination law is limited. This means that inexperienced panels will not find it easy to draw out pertinent practice recommendations. There is then a strong argument in favour of enabling panels to make a recommendation that an employer should consult with the EOC for advice on how to improve its policies and practices so as to avoid further instances of discrimination.

It is clear that most of the changes introduced by employers consequent to a tribunal finding have not been brought about as a result of recommendations. Few cases resulted in recommendations and the impact of these was limited. It may be that the process of fact finding and analysis in which the tribunal engages is likely to be of greater consequence than the specific findings and remedies proposed. Ultimately it will be desirable for the management of the organisation to be persuaded and convinced of the value and benefits of any changes which may prove necessary. This is likely to be best accomplished if management comes to an appreciation and understanding of the mechanisms which permitted the discrimination to occur. The skill with which the applicant's case is put together and argued may well be crucial to the development of such an appreciation.

Leonard has commented on those aspects of being represented which contribute to the complainant's success:

> ...a more precise explanation of representatives' success is probably their level of knowledge of equality legislation, which is complex and unique, as well as their knowledge and experience of tribunal procedure and case presentation[4].

It may well be that an employer will be more likely to take corrective action following a successful complain if the process has contributed to his understanding of equality legislation and the nature of the discrimination. Expertise in the preparation of cases may be compared in the cases against Frinkley Council (P6) and City Council (P1), which from a reading of the lengthy decisions were both well-presented and resulted in well-reasoned decisions, and both of which resulted in the organisation modifying its practices in progressive ways, with the less exhaustive assessment carried out by the tribunal in the cases against Foodcheck (R7) and Forward Enterprises (R1) which, despite the obvious scope for improvement, prompted no significant change in employment practices.

This highlights the need for good standards of advocacy and case presentation since without these an inexperienced panel is unlikely to be able to unfold by itself the context within which the applicant's claim arose. Skilful advocacy should improve the panel's understanding of the issues and thereby its reasoning capacities. In turn, a clear and intelligent presentation of the arguments by the panel should enable an employer to come to an appreciation of the failings, omissions and pitfalls in its current practices.

Frinkley Council (P6) and City Council (P1) have already been mentioned as examples of instances where such an appreciation came about. At least some managers in other organisations (Easterly RHA (P7), Homebuild Association (P10), Government Department (P11) and, to a lesser degree, Jones Outlets (R22)) were persuaded by the analysis of the panel.

This emphasis we have given to the process of case development and presentation as a way of improving the employer's understanding of the issues does not imply that remedy and penalty are unimportant. While it is unlikely that an employer can be induced to develop non-discriminatory practices merely through being required to pay a large amount of compensation to the applicant, evidence has been presented that employers who have been required to pay only very small amounts of compensation not only fail to engage in follow-up action, but also regard the tribunal process with disrespect, if not outright disdain. The cases we have examined in this study were all decided before the important case of *Alexander* v. *the Home Office*, a case of racial discrimination in which the Court of Appeal substituted an award for injury to feelings of £50 with an award of £500, and laid down guidelines for damages in discrimination cases. If, following the *Alexander* decision, the level of awards is generally raised, it may be that employers will not be quite as dismissive of tribunal proceedings as many now are.

Compensation is not a matter which has been central to our presentation of case study findings, although from the applicant's perspective it may be crucial. It has been difficult to judge the effect of a particular award in contributing to changed employment practices: awards have in general been low and one would need a group of cases with higher awards for proper comparison.

To use the industrial tribunal process only as a vehicle for resolving individual cases of employment discrimination is clearly of limited value. Its potential is much greater but remains largely undeveloped. We have shown in this r·search (see again Table 5) that some employers were encouraged to review policies and procedures through tribunal decisions, but it can be argued that more would have done so if awards were higher, if cases were better argued, if tribunals were better informed on discrimination matters, and if tribunals had powers to make more general recommendations and used their existing powers more often.

There is not much evidence to indicate that an isolated tribunal decision will by itself have enormous repercussions. However, if the organisation or a section of it is favourably disposed to promoting equality of opportunity within the organisation, and if the case is followed up either by a trade union, by the applicant or by the EOC, the tribunal decision can act as a building block or starting point for further activity. Our judgement, therefore, is that the industrial tribunal can and does play an important part in an overall strategy for bringing about employment equality. We further judge that the limited resources that currently go into promoting tribunal cases, for the most part trade union or EOC resources, should not be diverted to other activities, be they general investigations (in the case of the EOC) or to other campaigning or educational work. On the contrary, it is likely that industrial tribunals would have greater impact on employment practices if more resources could be put into case preparation and advocacy either through an extension of legal aid to applicants, or through a substantial increase in the funds available to the EOC to assist applicants legally, or through trade unions becoming more active in supporting sex discrimination applicants. Legal assistance and advice to applicants in industrial tribunal cases not only increases the applicant's chances of success, but is also likely to increase the chances of follow-up action by the employer as a more informed level of argument is made available about the employer's obligations, responsibilities, omissions and failures.

The EOC could do more to follow up tribunal decisions. A decision in favour of the applicant provides an opportunity for intervention which is not often taken even in cases which have been legally assisted by the EOC. The tribunal decision provides an opportunity for the EOC to take a closer interest in the affairs of the employer. This need not be a heavy-handed intervention. The EOC could make available to employers found to be in breach of equality legislation the offer of advice and assistance in the development of equal opportunity policies. Some employers may not need that advice and may be able to draw on other sources for practice development, but an awareness that the EOC is taking an interest could add impetus to the employer's own voluntary initiatives. At present, our judgement is that limited resources are put into providing legal assistance to applicants in order to improve their prospects of winning cases, but even fewer resources are devoted to pursuing with the implications of the employer losing the case.

Notes
1. Leonard, 1987b.
2. Leonard, 1986, p.31.
3. Dickens, et al, 1985, pp.268-269.
4. Leonard, 1987c, p.20.

Table 5 Summary of effects and changes

Case No	Name	(a) attitudes	(b) set-up EO policy	(c) reviewed existing EO policy	(d) action against discriminator	(e) specific practice changes
R1	Denton Council	better	x			
R2	Jones Outlets	worse	x			x
R3	Forward Enterprises	no change				
R4	Northern Tools	worse				
R5	Bolton Contracts	no change				x
R6	Camley Council	better				x
R7	Foodcheck Ltd	no change				x
R8	Paper Supply Co	no change				
P1	City Council	better	x			x
P2	Carlton Council	no change	x			x
P3	Power Supplies	no change			x	
P4	Surley Council	no change				x
P5	Shepley Transport	no change			x	
P6	Frinkley Council	better	x			x
P7	Easterly RHA	better	x			
P8	Ford Council	no change	x		x	x
P9	Popham Plastics	no change				
P10	Homebuild Association	better	x			
P11	Government Department	no change				x

Table 5 Summary of effects and changes (continued)

Case No	Name	(a) attitudes	(b) set-up EO policy	(c) reviewed existing EO policy	(d) action against discriminator	(e) specific practice changes
D1	Dinkworth	no change			x	x
D2	Woodgate	no change				
D3	Trust Centre	no change		x		x
D4	Government Department	better		x		x
D5	Chorley Motors	no change				
D6	Carelle Kitchens	no change				
D7	Wellmade Brick Co	no change				
D8	Samson	no change				
D9	Clearways Trust	no change				
E1	Browns Ltd	no change			x	x
E2	Starpress Ltd	worse				
E3	Northside Dealers	no change				x
E4	Butcher Engineering	no change				x
E5	Craft Castings	worse				x
E6	Hilling Council	worse				
E7	Chestertons	no change				
E8	Higgins International	no change				
E9	New World Schools	no change				
E10	Motorbox	no change				
E11	Wellmans	no change				
E12	Grants Builders	no change				

Table 6   Summary of specific practice changes

R2	**Jones Outlets**	procedures for giving out job application forms altered
R5	**Boltons Contracts**	decision sent to managers and implications outlined in memo; case used in training
R6	**Camley Council**	drafted new practice notes on recruitment methods; new recruitment manual introduced
R7	**Foodcheck**	*decision notified to other area managers but unlikely to have been consequent changes*
P1	**City Council**	Circular issued on new maternity leave arrangements; general improvements in personnel procedures
P2	**Carlton Council**	HQ took over the running of certain promotion boards; composition of promotion boards changed
P4	**Surley Council**	*copy of IT decision and circular issued to departmental heads giving advice on conduct of interviews; practice on taking up references clarified*
P6	**Frinkley Council**	officers instructed to intervene more at interview/ promotion boards; notes ordered to be kept of interviews
P8	**Ford Council**	circular sent to all Chief Officers on selection and interview procedures
P11	**Government Department**	decision used in negotiating wider agreement with POA; new arrangements on opposite sex postings introduced
D1	**Dinkworth**	*personnel procedures revised and improved;* procedures for dismissal of employees changed
D3	**Trust Centre**	*more formal recruitment procedures introduced*
D4	**Government Department**	extension of part-time job opportunities; job-share register introduced; leaflet issued
E1	**Browns**	new pay scheme introduced with assistance of ACAS
E3	**Northside**	pay of reception staff harmonised; another female employee up-graded
E4	**Butcher**	*consultant brought in to advise on pay structure*
E5	**Craft Casings**	*procedure for red-circling of jobs changed*

References

Department of Employment, 1987, *Employment Gazette*, October.

Equal Opportunities Commission, 1988, *Equal Treatment for Men and Women, Strengthening the Acts: Formal Proposals*.

Dickens, L., Jones, M., Weekes, B., Hart, M., 1985, *Dismissed: A Study of Unfair Dismissal and the Industrial Tribunal System*, Blackwell.

Leonard, A.M.,

1986, *The First Eight Years: A Profile of Applicants to the Industrial Tribunals under the Sex Discrimination and Equal Pay Acts, 1976-1983*, EOC
1987a, *Judging Inequality: effectiveness of the industrial tribunal system in sex discrimination and equal pay cases*, Cobden Trust
1987b, *Pyrrhic Victories: winning sex discrimination and equal pay cases in the industrial tribunals, 1980-1984*, HMSO
1987c, Judging Inequality, *Equal Opportunities Review*, No.16

Rubinstein, M., 1988, Creating a Virtuous Circle: the new case law and its implications, *Equal Opportunities Review*, No.20.